Colin Od

The Pocket Essential

VAMPIRE FILMS

www.pocketessentials.com

First published in Great Britain 2000 by Pocket Essentials, 18 Coleswood Road,
Harpenden, Herts, AL5 1EQ

Distributed in the USA by Trafalgar Square Publishing, P.O. Box 257, Howe Hill Road,
North Pomfret, Vermont 05053

A CIP catalogue record for this book is available from the British Library.

ISBN 1-903047-17-X

9 8 7 6 5 4 3 2 1

Book typeset by Lies
Printed and bound by Cox & Wyman

for Mum and Dad and Mum

Acknowledgements

Huge thanks to everyone who helped us satisfy our insatiable lust for all things vampiric: The Superalmagamated John Ashbrook, Lucia Goodwin, Paul and Elizabeth Billinger, Anthony (just call me Bruce) Fawcett, Paul Duncan, Richard King and the friendly folk from Screen Edge, Lynn from Medusa Communications, Entertainment in Video and Pete Tombs. For his advice on vampire lore and legend, salutations to the inscrutable Leonard Fell. Thanks to Elizabeth Billinger for doing clever money stuff. Thanks to Meike Benzler and Jim de Liscard for lashings of enthusiasm. And to all our friends and family who have been neglected throughout the writing of this book, sorry guys and thanks for all your support. Finally to Alice the purring predator, who sleeps by day, and sleeps by night too.

Contents

1. Pleasures And Wayward Distractions

I felt the hot molten pierce of the stare, the whirlpool of the eyes. The veins in my neck strained to be near those pearly harbingers of death, that hungry tongue, the ruby lips. Trembling in anticipation, bursting with desire, I submitted myself to the warm embrace of oblivion...

The many guises of the undead continue to hypnotise audiences the world over and vampires have long held a particular fascination, reinvented and rediscovered by each generation to mirror their fears and desires. They are, above all else, adaptable. The zombie repels, its lack of personality leaves little room for exposition so its role is to represent the fear of the faceless mass. Similarly the werewolf, a staple of folklore, represents a lack of control over man's predatory nature - its horror lies in the loss of free will. The vampire, on the other hand, is a far more malleable creature that allows for the projection of human fears and desires without confronting the actuality. As 'supernatural' beings they offer escape from reality and an opportunity to encounter evil in the safe environment of the cinema. Not, of course, that all vampires are evil - some are cursed, tragic, funny or just different - it is their exaggeration and extension of human feelings and abilities that allows them to be reinterpreted.

As long as there has been cinema there has been censorship and vampires. The vampire provides an ideal forum for exploring taboo subjects in a metaphorical context, allowing situations that would be considered unacceptable if one or more of the participants were not nosferatu. To this end the more successful vampire films have often been made in oppressive or puritanical environments. The cinematic evolution of the vampire takes on the issues and mores of its time - even if it is a period piece. You will find no difficulty spotting the difference between *Brides Of Dracula* and *Countess Dracula* despite the fact they are made at the same location by the same company. The contemporary concerns and attitudes of the audience changes the perception of both the vampire and its slayer. *Blacula* has a suave but hip vampire, *Vamp* a sexually predatory female and Frank Langella makes a bodice-ripper *Dracula*. *Buffy* has teenage problems to contend with as well as the undead, *Fright Night* has a post-*Porky's* 80s disco guy punished for voyeurism while *Captain Kronos, Vampire Hunter* is a totally British combination of Errol Flynn and *The Avengers*!

Where there are vampires there are usually vampire hunters. These can be as amoral (James Woods in *Vampires*) or sadistic (Peter Cushing in *Twins Of Evil*) as their prey - often hiding behind religious fanaticism as an excuse for their excesses and violations. In many cases, their sadism is a sign of repressed sexuality or fascistic devotion. With few exceptions (Buffy, Captain Kronos) they are far more pompous and dull than their nemeses. Puritanism generally relies on the exorcism of the vampire by the film's close - it is the resumption of order that provides the audience with the opportunity of having their cake and eating it. They can identify with the bohemian free sexuality and ego of the monster, but be safe walking home knowing that they are not going to be the victim of what they want to be. To this end the vampire hunter must necessarily be dull and represent authority.

Themes

The diversity of the vampire means that it is rich for analysis. Akin to its position as a breaker of taboos the thematic streams of the vampire film can appear contradictory. This is its strength. Often serving as a metaphor, the viewer can engage with the film-maker in any number of metaphysical or social discourses within the relative comfort of a traditional narrative form. This is not to say that the majority of vampire films are worthy philosophical texts but their versatility allows for additional layers beneath the surface, should the viewer require it, even in the most basic film. With such a long and rich history it should come as no surprise that these arguments can often work both ways - one film-maker's 'vampire as fear of fascism' is another's 'vampire as fear of communism.' Below are a few of the key themes, there are many, many more.

Disease

Vampirism is transmittable through the exchange of blood/bodily fluids. You can become 'contaminated' with it. The relationship between the vampire and the plague carrier is a complex one. On one hand you can view the vampire as bestowing the disease/gift of immortality. Or because the recipient is (sometimes) turned through the mutual exchange of fluids, the victim is complicit in his/her own downfall. The vampire may contaminate just because of its feeding habits. This is not conducive to the overall survival of the vampire species, due to exponential rise in population and the inevitable decline in foodstock. The relationship between vampires and disease is a long one. Dracula is associated with rats in the novel and films, most explicitly in Murnau's version. The town in *Vampire Circus* is isolated by the plague - its appearance is a precursor for vampiric revenge. A far more common metaphor is made in films of the last two decades, which relate vampirism and AIDS (*Sucker The Vampire*).

Sexuality

The continued fascination of British and American audiences with vampires has a lot to do with the repression of sexuality within these cultures - vampires often provide a safe way of confronting eroticism. In times when even married couples were denied on-screen embraces, you could still see a seductive vampire break into the bedroom of a swooning woman. The act of biting and sucking bodily fluids itself is extremely sexual, but usually depicted with implication, subtlety and ritual. Once again, taboos can be addressed in a safe environment. Films like *Daughter Of Dracula* were surprisingly frank in their depiction of lesbian seduction and any of Dracula's nocturnal visits could be considered fantasies about extra-marital sex. Later films toyed with further concepts of what could be considered deviant sexual practices. The thing that sets these films apart from pornography is that their perversions are implied or at least restrained. Despite the delirious fetishism and rampant nudity of many European vampire films in the 60s and 70s, the genre declined significantly with the brief mainstream acceptance of hard-core pornography. For all their taboo confrontation the vampire seemed antiquated and even, heaven forbid, wholesome. The erotic appeal of the vampire is in the danger, the taboo and the promise of sex, not the act itself.

Bourgeois/Aristocracy Vs The Herd

Dracula/Vlad, Elizabeth Bathory - nobility. Powerful and aristocratic, they represent the vampire as royalty, superior, commanding their subjects to do their bidding. No one cared when pretty virgin girls disappeared for Bathory's vanity or when Vlad dined among the corpses of his enemies, they were either peasants or foreigners. The decadence of vampires is legendary. When these ways are challenged though, they reflect the impetuosity of youth against bourgeois conservatism. In *Blade*, the young vampires seek to overthrow those of pure lineage - they are the mob against the nobility. In this example the new is seen, paradoxically, as bad - the Elders have survived by limiting numbers and remaining withdrawn from general view - preferring to manipulate from afar. In Abel Ferrera's *The Addiction* there is a vein of grunge Nazism running through the vampire circle. Ferrera's left-wing approach to film-making sees his undead as the modern Nazi.

Opposite side of the same coin is the fear of the communist takeover, although this is less common in the vampire film and more prevalent in the faceless mass of the zombie picture. *Blade* sees both groups represented, the ultimate goal for the new nosferatu is to introduce vampirism to the entire world. In *The Omega Man,* the last man on earth stakes vampires by day and hides by night - he is the outsider, the individual facing the horde.

Fear Of Death/Growing Old

Death, by definition, plays a key role in the genre. Fear of death, longing for death, fear of growing old, immortality. The vampire's connection with the afterlife is complex and manyfold. Because of religion the vampire is damned - not alive but as yet unjudged, whose every move takes them further from Heaven and closer to Hell. For others the promise of eternal youth sees vampirism as an elixir. *The Lost Boys* embraces this concept. The problem with eternal life is a life on the move, watching loved ones grow old and die (*The Hunger*), until the very thing you avoided becomes your only wish (*Requiem For The Vampire*). For others the pain of seeing loved ones live again is too much - some vampire films come to terms with death by offering a worse alternative to it (Lucy Harker's rebirth), eternal slavery without love or redemption. Age is something that troubles most of us at some time. The vampire offers a solution to this by remaining ever young. This creates its own problems. In *Countess Dracula*, Ingrid Pitt's Elizabeth Bathory needs to kill in order to stay beautiful. The same character in Harry Kumel's *Daughters Of Darkness* preys on the young to become her companion. She never suffers the inevitable ravages of age. Not only do vampires cheat death, they also cheat the effects of life.

Sources

Much of the inspiration behind vampire films derives directly from literature and legend. Polidori's *The Vampyre* was only a short story, but its antagonist Lord Ruthven (allegedly modelled on Lord Byron) was an origin of the dark, compelling and yet strangely attractive aristocrat, upon which so many screen vampires fashioned themselves. Similarly J Sheridan Le Fanu's *Carmilla,* the beautiful, mysterious seductress has appeared in several films in various guises. A Russian story *The Family Of The Vourdalouk* by Alexis Tolstoy has provided the inspiration for several (normally European) films. The legendary Elizabeth (Erzsebet) Bathory of Hungary bathed in the blood of virgins in order to maintain her youth, allegedly killing some 600 young girls. She too has been represented many times. Of all the myths and stories from which vampire films have drawn, the most influential is undoubtedly that of *Dracula* created by Bram Stoker.

Dracula

So many films have been made about the Count that an entire Pocket Essential could be filled on that subject alone. Of the many actors that have depicted the Count, two have become immortal: Bela Lugosi and Christopher Lee. Despite the fact that they were enormously talented actors in other fields, both became famous simply for being Dracula. Lugosi, who was responsible for creating the classic swishing cape and slicked back hair, first appeared in Tod Browning's *Dracula* (1931) having already played the role on the stage. It was to become his trademark. Lugosi's Dracula was compelling - his hand gestures would hypnotise and draw his victims to him, his accent exotic and tempting. It is no wonder that he received sacks of fan mail from adoring women. However, the studios did not know how to handle his talents, so they rejected him. His subsequent spiral into drug addiction and debt was nothing short of tragic. Christopher Lee, tall, imposing and with blood red eyes became another classic embodiment of the Count. His presence alone was normally enough to control his victims although, if he had to escape from a slayer, he could also hotfoot it pretty damned quickly. Most noted for his roles in Hammer films, he also played Dracula elsewhere, such as *Uncle Was A Vampire* (Italy 1959), *Count Dracula* (1970), the documentary *In Search Of Dracula* (1972), and *Dracula And Son* (1976).

John Carradine appeared in hundreds of films, his horror work was but a small portion of his lengthy career. He too depicted Dracula on several occasions, a white-haired and moustached individual, with top hat and tails in *House Of Frankenstein* (1944) and *House Of Dracula* (1945). He went on to appear in *Billy The Kid Vs Dracula* (1965) amongst many others, continuing in *Nocturna, Granddaughter Of Dracula* (1973), aged 73. Other Counts have included a dapper Lon Chaney Jr in *Son Of Dracula* (1943) and Francis Lederer in *The Return Of Count Dracula* (1958). Everyone's favourite Van Helsing, Peter Cushing turned to vampirism in *Tendre Dracula* (1973) and even donned a Bela Lugosi cape. Jack Palance was a tormented and bitter *Dracula* (1973), Louis Jourdan in *Count Dracula* (1973) initiated a smoother, creepier depiction and Frank Langella continued as a suave but vaguely repellent Count in the 1979 version.

Klaus Kinski was *Nosferatu* in 1979, all bald horror and sharp incisors, reprising Max Schreck's seminal performance in Murnau's classic. Gary Oldman gave yet another interpretation in 1992's *Bram Stoker's Dracula* and tried to emphasise the tragic nature of the Count's existence as well as linking him with the historical figure of Vlad Tepes.

There have been too many more films based on Dracula to mention. Like all vampires, he is highly adaptable, hence these derivatives. Be warned, we offer absolutely no guarantees about quality: *Count Erotica, Vampire* (1971), *Dragula* (1973), *Spermula* (1975), *Deafula* (1975) in sign language, *Gayracula* (1983), *Trampire* (1987), *Rockula* (1990).

Using This Book

The sheer bulk of vampire films means that this book would have ended up a list had we mentioned every one. Instead we have produced a history, covered various sub-genres and introduced flavours of vampirism from around the world. If we have missed your all time favourite, then we apologise. We have focussed generally on films which are easily obtainable, hopefully you'll find some tempting and tantalising morsels within...

2. Early Morsels

Whatever its merits as a novel the effects of *Dracula* on the history of vampire films is immense, so it is fitting therefore that the birth of Stoker's tome coincided with that of cinema itself. The first film that can loosely be termed a vampire film was Mélies *Le Manoir Du Diable* (1896), made while Stoker was finishing his novel. Mélies was cinema's pioneering magician relying heavily on in-camera special effects to show the impossible to his astonished audience. *Le Manoir Du Diable* features a flying bat transforming into a demonic figure played by Mélies himself. Running in at 2 minutes there is, of course, no time for characterisation but it is appropriate that film's first showman was also its first vampire. Sadly much of early cinema is lost, disappearing in a wisp of nitrate or through neglect and war. France produced *Les Vampires* (1916) a sensationalist crime serial directed by Louis Feuillade, a prolific producer of over 800 films and series including the supernatural Raffles-style character *Fantômas* (1913-4). Despite featuring a number of bizarre characters (including the all-seeing Grand Vampire and the sinister Satanas) during its convoluted succession of shocking abductions, the series is best remembered for its black-suited anti-heroine Irma Vep (portrayed with black-lipped melodramatic intensity by Musidora - the character name an anagram of vampire). Eschewing what we now understand as narrative cinema for free-form association, the series proved to be a huge influence on the surrealist directors of the 1920s and years later Jean Rollin and Olivier Assayas.

France was not alone in vampire production, the US were making the popular weekly serials to ensure repeat audience attendance. *The Exploits Of Elaine* (1915) features a character called The Clutching Hand who tries to drink our sassy heroine's blood by attacking her with a hypodermic, predating Romero's *Martin* by some 60 years. The UK produced *The Great London Mystery* (1920) featuring the intriguingly named Froggie the Vampire. Hungary had been producing horror films for some time and eventually turned their hand to Stoker - *Drakula* (1921) is the first adaptation of the book but is lost to the world. The following year saw Murnau's landmark *Nosferatu* (1922). Back in the US, Tod Browning, who was once a 'Living Hypnotic Corpse' circus side-show attraction, and the great horror actor Lon Chaney filmed *London After Midnight* (1927) for MGM. Browning would return to vampires with *Dracula* (1930), still the most famous of Stoker adaptations.

Nosferatu (1921, Germany)

Director: FW Murnau

Starring: Max Schreck, Alexander Granach

Young solicitor Jonathon Harker bids farewell to his wife Nina, and sets off for Dracula's castle. Dracula wishes to purchase a property in Bremen, notices Harker's portrait of Nina and sets off to find her. On his arrival, a mysterious curse afflicts the town. Dracula seeks Nina, who has now been reunited with her husband. Fortunately Jonathan was given a book about Nosferatu so they prepare to deal with the escalating undead menace.

This is one of the first adaptations of Stoker's *Dracula*, indeed so similar to the book that Stoker's widow successfully sued the production company and ordered the prints to be destroyed. Fortunately, some survived and this remains one of the most influential vampire films of all time. From the mad Carpathian peasants to the spooky carriage which takes Harker to the castle and the marvellous use of shadows, it established the conventions upon which so many future films would rely, with one exception - that of Dracula himself. Played by Max Schreck, this Count is a monster. When we first encounter him as Harker arrives at the castle, he appears to be a thin, wizened old man in black suit and hat. However, as we realise who he is, his appearance becomes increasingly grotesque - tall, thin, bald with bat-like ears, enormous claw-like hands and sharp pointed teeth. Very few subsequent vampires followed this model (the 1979 remake and *Salem's Lot* being the only notable examples). However, despite his shocking appearance and creepy mannerisms, some degree of sympathy awakens in the viewer. Looking from his window longingly for Nina, he creeps about hunched, a figure of shame. The film's style is marvellous and reflects much of the German expressionist movement of the time. The menacing shadows (particularly those as Dracula creeps up to Nina), close-ups of rats wriggling from the coffins. and the glimpses of Dracula's teeth through the rotting coffin lid still have the power to unnerve.

60min, PG, Redemption, Fang Factor Four.

Vampyr: Der Traum des Allan Grey (1931, Germany)

Dir: Carl Dreyer

St: Julian West

Anthropologist David Grey (despite the film's title card) arrives at the town of Courtempierre. He is given a package by a babbling old man. Before long David discovers that Leone, the girl in the bedroom above him, appears very sick. When David opens the package he is perturbed by the message to "free us from our affliction." Is this connected with Marguerite Chopin, an infamous witch and her burial in an unhallowed grave? With Leone's condition worsening, David is called in by a strangely nocturnal doctor to supply blood for a transfusion but events get increasingly hallucinatory and he begins to worry for his sanity, and his soul.

In 1930 Carl Dreyer was one of the world's most highly-respected directors and at the height of his critical success. Then, in a suicidal career move, he made a horror film which, you see, was not art. Dreyer, however, thought differently and set about adapting Le Fanu's *In A Glass Darkly* as a dreamlike tale of madness and dark brooding horror. It was a far cry from accepted Hollywood conventions of linear narrative and coherent structured dialogue. Dreyer's is a world of half-heard words, whispers, changes of language, animal yelps, children crying, uncertainty. If structurally, aurally and conceptually the film seeks to represent surrealist ideas, it is within the visual element that this is consolidated. The film's use of imagery is astonishing with each shot adding psychological depth and heightened unease to the proceedings - shadows of bats are cast behind characters, cruciform beams of light pick out details and the village is overseen by a macabre weathervane of an impaled witch. Scythe-carrying peasants meander in half light, menacing sextons are constantly shown in shadow and the whole piece is made with such an air of putrefied menace that it is easy to see why the film was witch-hunted. Hollywood was producing little more than fairy tales in comparison. Chief source of outrage was reserved for the astonishing dream sequence where David finds himself in a glass-topped coffin, unable to scream. We follow his journey from undertakers to burial in chilling point of view as faces leer over him, the lid is slowly screwed down and his perverse fate dragged out. The film was condemned and sadly most surviving prints are of very poor quality - an unfortunate fate for an unconventional and daring work by a master filmmaker.

52min, PG, Redemption, Fang Factor Four.

Dracula (1930, USA)

Dir: Tod Browning
St: Bela Lugosi, Dwight Frye, David Manners, Helen Chandler

Renfield travels to Transylvania to sell Carfax Abbey to the upwardly mobile Count Dracula. Terrorised by three ghostly brides, Dracula makes him subservient to his will and, quite mad, he is incarcerated in Dr Seward's home. Dr Seward and his daughter Mina meet Dracula at the opera, unaware that he has an unusual disposition when it comes to necks - a fact later borne by Mina's friend Lucy's sudden death. Soon attacks on children by a woman in white and increasing weirdness at the neighbour's house begins to raise eyebrows, especially with resident stake-bearer Abraham Van Helsing.

The success and influence of Browning's *Dracula* is so immense that it can be difficult to view it with real objectivity. It is easy to spot the film's origins as a stage play. Lugosi wasn't the first choice, he was quite a way down a list that included Conrad Veidt and Lon Chaney Snr, but ultimately the Hungarian born actor was made for the part. Even if the accentuated lighting occasionally misses the mark, Lugosi draws the eye with raw power and considerable charm - when he attacks men he is a savage, for women he is a passionate lover. Browning's apathy towards the project is sporadically clear - individual sequences remain powerful and affecting even now, but large scenes of dialogue-heavy exposition and off-screen action seem lazy. Dracula was filmed prior to the onslaught of the Hayes Code which restricted much of what had become normal on screen - Lugosi's bedroom antics would have been toned down significantly otherwise. What is remarkable is the attention to set detail, particularly in Dracula's Castle, it really makes you wonder why he'd want to move! A huge cathedral-like hall with streaming light, a dizzying staircase, gargantuan spiders webs and Lugosi intoning "I am Dracula" - it can only go downhill. There are so many ideas at the start - the bat leading the coach, the diffuse lit brides stalking Renfield, the unexpected appearance of the aardvarks - that Browning has run out of steam by the time they take the Vesta to England with only a stalking Renfield delivering any chills in the next hour. While Browning was shooting his film, Universal commissioned George Melford to simultaneously shoot a Spanish version with Carlos Villarias as Dracula, using the same sets with apparently far better results.

84min, PG, CIC Video, Fang Factor Two.

The Vampire Bat (1933, USA)

Dir: Frank Strayer
St: Lionel Atwill, Fay Wray, Melvyn Douglas

Kleinschloss, a "village in terror" awaits another vampire murder. Karl and Ruth suspects the deaths are the result of a murderer but the village folk think differently. The suspect is clear - the retarded Herman has been seen at the bedsides of the victims and, what's more, he collects bats. Incensed by Herman's oddness, the town form a posse, chase him and stake him, just to be sure. But will this drastic action stop the appalling killings, the "lifeless skeletons of flesh and bone," or is there a more chilling solution?

A film of two halves which, unfortunately, are jumbled up. On one hand there is the invasive and impressive prowling camerawork that glides like a dreaming bat and then there are the static stagy routines that are starkly lit and flat. The film's message is that ignorance kills and science kills - Herman may well be unbalanced but his fascination with the huge bats that impressively dominate the exterior shots is understandable - they are furry. His hounding by the villagers and ultimate demise are moving and futile. Science is shown to be the pursuit of knowledge at the expense of others, blind even if it is coldly logical. The final revelations are unexpected, the ideas surprisingly literate but the film feels obliged to end it all on a Nathan Smith/Fu Manchu note with elaborate torture/medical set-ups and a few pulp-blazing guns. The acting ranges from superb to melodramatic and unfortunately Wray is woefully underused. Aunt Guthy, a loopy hypochondriac with an impressive knowledge of ailments, provides some comic relief but does irritate. Tight, with a flowery but likeable script, *The Vampire Bat* passes a pleasant hour.

60min, PG, Redemption, Fang Factor Two and a Half.

Mark Of The Vampire (1935, USA)

Dir: Tod Browning

St: Lionel Barrymore, Lionel Atwill, Bela Lugosi, Elizabeth Allan

In a creepy Czechoslovakian village, the herb bat-thorn keeps the creatures of the night from disrupting their fragile existence. When Sir Karell shuffles of his mortal coil, found with two puncture wounds in his neck and a surprisingly low plasma count, his sceptical daughter and son-in-law-to-be are suddenly concerned. With the servants running all over the house like mad things and nocturnal visits from a very strange couple, they are clearly in need of professional help. As luck would have it Inspector Neumann is on the case, helped by hypnotist "The Professor." So that's alright then...

In 1927 Tod Browning made a vampire film called *London After Midnight* with the first great horror actor Lon Chaney, a one-man franchise, who created and applied all his own horrific make-up. For *London After Midnight* he fashioned a set of canine incisors that stretched his mouth into a deadly grotesque grin of razor sharp points. It remains the most sought after of all vampire films. Before a decade had passed Browning was to remake it as *The Mark Of The Vampire*, reunited with Dracula stalwart Bela Lugosi at the height of his acting abilities.

Although some of the dialogue scenes are a little staid, the sheer bravura of the visual imagination leaves you breathless. From the opening shot of a crucifix church-top bleeding light, to the eerie graveyards and tombs you can cut the atmosphere. What the Count's castle lacks in the physical dimensions to his Transylvanian abode, it more than makes up for in decor - intricate spiders webs, chandeliers, candles, old pianos and coffins. Huge spiders scuttle along the walls, insects scurry around the drapes and vampire bats squawk around. It is incredible, even more so because of Wong Howe's sumptuous cinematography and some quite remarkable special effects. In one sequence we see Count Mora's marble white bride drift slowly to the ground, her outstretched arms like the wings of a giant bat - awe inspiring and beautiful. These "demons of the castle" that are "spewed up from the grave" manage to terrorise effortlessly and silently. The mood would be perfect were it not for a couple of niggling points - first, any character named Otto is bound to be shifty and secondly, whilst the final revelations are unexpected and inventive, they do end matters on a sensible note.

Fang Factor Four.

Dracula's Daughter (1936, USA)

Dir: Lambert Hillyer
St: Gloria Holden, Otto Kruger, Marguerite Churchill

Dracula is dead and Van Helsing up on a murder rap for staking the Count - it's either the gallows or the asylum for him. Unless. Wait! Dracula is corpse-napped by the beautiful black-cloaked figure of Marya Zaleska who burns him with a purifying flame to release his power over her. This attempt to curtail her nocturnal yearnings for human blood prove in vain, as do her endeavours to try piano playing or painting. Instead she needs to return to Transylvania to confront the roots of her problem.

Universal's follow-up to the hugely successful *Dracula* is a far more satisfying and low-key affair. Running in at less than seventy minutes, the script crackles with pace and energy, so lean there's hardly room to breathe - not that you need to if you're undead. It is also one of the earliest examples of knowingly Freudian cinema, at once embracing psychoanalytic ideas and pointing out their weaknesses, or as Marya puts it "There are more things in Heaven and Earth than are dreamt of in your psychiatry." Dr Garth's attempt to prevent Marya's "horrible impulses" by putting them in a psychological context, and the authority's treatment of Van Helsing as a murderer rather than hero, place the film in a highly believable context. Also surprising are the distinctly lesbian overtones that accompany Marya's feeding on Lili, and her subsequent responsibility for the girl. The offering of eternal life to the object of her affection rather than her faithful but facetious servant speaks volumes about her blind love. Marya is a tragic and complex figure who does not want to feed. As such she is a precursor for Rollin's *The Living Dead Girl* as someone whose primitive instincts displace their conscience - "There is nothing ahead for me but horror." *Dracula's Daughter* has worn the ravages of time very well, it is now at pension age. Despite the occasional scene being filmed with an overly static camera, the uniformly excellent acting and rich dialogue carry it through - even the British Bobbies are realistic and not Hollywood 'Mockneys.' Essential watching.

Riding high on the success of this film, Universal launched a new movie where Lon Chaney Jr played the 'subtly' named Count Alucard in Robert

Siodmak's *Son Of Dracula*. Further sequels were spawned - *House Of Frankenstein* (1944) and *House Of Dracula* (1945).

68min, PG, CIC Video, Fang Factor Four.

The Return Of The Vampire (1943, USA)

Dir: Lew Landers
St: Bela Lugosi, Frieda Inescort

London. 23 years ago Lady Jane helped put a sharp end to Armand Tesla's reign of terror, freeing wolfman servant Andreas and narrowly avoiding little Nicki being the next victim. Now, the German Blitzkrieg disturbs the graves in Priory cemetery, and Tesla reappears, adopting the persona of a visiting scientist as Nicki prepares for her engagement party. The authorities will have none of this supernatural gobbledegook so it is left to Lady Jane to thwart the tide of evil once more.

The poignant backdrop of war-ravaged London with the maintenance of stiff upper lip Britishness contrasts neatly with the supernatural absurdity of the base premise. The denial of accepting that Tesla is still alive holds back the authorities - at one point they consider exhuming him and charging Lady Jane for murder! The cemetery design is wonderful, as is the fog spilling into the bedrooms of Tesla's victims mirroring his macabre resting places. Sadly though, Andreas the wolfman looks like a cross between the lion in *The Wizard Of Oz* and Chewbacca, presumably to make him more sympathetic. There's ample comic relief provided by two 'luv-a-duck' gravediggers but in the end you are left with a competent film nicely shot (the opening raven is fabulous) and little more.

Fang Factor Two and a (wolf) hairs breadth.

3. Hurrah For Hammer

The name of Hammer Studios is so inexorably linked with the British horror film that even now, nearly a quarter of a century after their last feature production, the term Hammer Horror is universally known. The company was started as a film distributor in 1937 and soon moving into production, generally providing the tail-ends of double bills and 'quota quickies.' After a brief hiatus during the war, they returned, seeking inspiration in radio shows such as *Dick Barton: Special Agent*. It wasn't long before they turned their eyes towards television adaptations. *The Quatermass Experiment* had been a successful and intelligent BBC series. Hammer honed it to the bone, made the central character American and

19

emphasised the 'X' in the title to push home the horrific aspects. The film was an unqualified success and paved the way for Hammer's golden age. *The Curse Of Frankenstein* followed and Hammer hit the big time - Terence Fisher's film was produced in glorious, blood-saturated Technicolor from a budget-conscious copyright-free source. Its period setting allowed for far more freedom in the sex and horror department than a contemporary one would have allowed and audiences responded appropriately. To consolidate their success, Hammer looked for another classic text to film and came up with *Dracula*. Re-teaming Cushing and Lee from *The Curse Of Frankenstein* allowed for greater audience association with the previous success, but they weren't prepared for Lee as such a sexually charged and dominating Count. Both films provided Hammer with a stable series base which continued throughout the 60s.

If the 60s were Hammer's heydays then the 70s were its death throes. Audiences had become 'sophisticated' and demanded more contemporary and visceral film-making. Attempts to update their product to appeal to hip, swinging kids proved embarrassing - the sexuality coy compared to that of our free-thinking European cousins and the violence lacking the gritty intensity of an America still in the grip of the Vietnam war. Suddenly it all seemed so damned British, but in reality it always was. Hammer floundered - only staying above water with British-only appeal successes such as *Mutiny On The Buses* and the lamentable *Love Thy Neighbour*. Hammer's last horror film was an effective Dennis Wheatley adaptation *To The Devil A Daughter*. Sadly it is unlikely that we will see another British studio of its ilk.

Firstly, the Dracula films....

Dracula (aka The Horror Of Dracula) (1958)

Dir: Terrence Fisher

St: Peter Cushing, Christopher Lee

Jonathan Harker, vampire slayer, has taken up a position as librarian at Dracula's castle. But before he can stake the evil one, he is turned nosferatu and his colleague Dr Van Helsing has to put him to rest. In the meantime, Dracula has vanished. Van Helsing travels to the Holmwood residence to inform Jonathan's fiancée Lucy of his sad demise. However, Lucy is gravely ill and her brother Arthur and his wife Mina are most concerned. Could there be some connection to Dracula's disappearance?

Forget the inconsistencies with Stoker's novel, they are irrelevant. This film is nothing short of a masterpiece. From the very opening - the castle in the woods now so familiar to fans, Lee's dramatic entrance as Dracula and Cushing's no nonsense Van Helsing - it contains all the ingredients of classic Hammer. The film takes horrific and erotic elements to extremes but they remain tightly contained within the restraints allowed by 50s Britain. Jonathan staking Dracula's consort, filmed as a dramatic shadow against the wall depicted nothing explicit, but still has the power to shock. Lucy, in her sickbed, tended by her sister in law is the very image of virtue and humility. As soon as everyone has gone though, her expression changes to one of wanton wickedness as she opens the windows and removes her crucifix awaiting the kiss of the vampire. It is unbelievably erotic, yet she is the only person in the scene. As a vampire, she becomes even more seductive and coquettish, only the stake can bring her peace. Fisher is a master of pacing, making full use of Jimmy Sangster's intelligent script. He takes his time when he needs to, allowing the comic scenes to break down the tension, but when Van Helsing finally realises where Dracula is, the thrill of the chase is astonishing. The final duel between Cushing and Lee is charged with energy - their expressions show sheer hatred as they battle to the death. Dracula's demise is shocking, his remains crumbling to dust amongst the best effects that Hammer produced. Marvellous.

78min, 15, Warner Home Video, Fang Factor Five.

Dracula: Prince Of Darkness (1965)

Dir: Terence Fisher

St: Christopher Lee, Barbara Shelley

Two English couples are on a tour of Europe. The local town's people are a twitchy superstitious lot who stake and burn anyone "just in case" but even towering cynical priest Father Shandor agrees that they really shouldn't go to visit Carlsbad. Do they listen? Of course not. Dumped by Eastern Europe's only cockney cabby, they take a driverless carriage to a castle. There they are greeted by the butler Clove and a warm dinner - "is your master indisposed?" asks Charles, "No, he's dead." Not for long though, Alan's death revives the Count and Helen receives a serious hicky. Charles and Diana (no sniggering) escape briefly but not for long.

Fisher's film is a real tease from start to finish, Dracula himself does not appear until the second half, but this is all part of the plan. British to the hilt, the trappings of a horror film are used to depict the allegorical effects of extra-marital liaisons and repressed sexuality. Helen is a frumpy wimp with an irritating husband. How much better she is when freed of the shackles of matrimony and heaving in a negligee for her demonic lover.

21

Diana is bubbly enough only to contemplate an affair with the undead. Charles is required to be macho but is essentially impotent, the real saviour coming in the shape of Father Shandor. Shandor is one of Hammer's finest characters, a rumbustious cleric devoid of social graces. Think Friar Tuck on steroids with a big gun. Mention must also be made of the phenomenal butler Clove, droll in a *Rocky Horror Show* way. With such an eclectic bunch of miscreants, Fisher can do no wrong, his use of widescreen Technicolor enhances the period feel, sweeping from costume drama to comic strip once the Count has risen again - the transformation of his castle alone by alteration in lighting is astonishing. The lack of action enhances the melodrama and dread, all accentuated by a superbly expansive score.

87min, 15, Warner Home Video, Fang Factor Four.

Taste The Blood Of Dracula (1969)

Dir: Peter Sasdy
St: Christopher Lee, Roy Kinear, Peter Sallis

Chubby salesman Weller has a very interesting item to sell - an urn containing the dried blood of Count Dracula. He peddles it to Lord Courtly, an impudent fellow bored with the endless stream of orgies and debauchery his position demands. Courtly tastes the blood, something his fellow scallywags are unimpressed by, so they duly kick him in. But wait! He turns into Dracula and seeks bloody vengeance on the hypocritical bunch and their families.

Upholding the moral high ground whilst enjoying the excesses is key to the hypocrisy of not only the town officials but also Hammer films as a whole. Alice is repressed because her father doesn't want her to have sex or even go out, while he's free to poke as many prostitutes as he fancies. That Alice does go out is punishable by being seduced and turned by Dracula himself. A horror film cliché, if you want a fighting chance of making it to the final credits then don't have sex. Where *Taste The Blood Of Dracula* succeeds is in the sheer delirium of the cast - it's like a grotesque pantomime with Ralph Bates in particular giving an outstanding over-the-top performance that makes even the excesses of the cast of TV familiars seem positively tame. As normal, this leaves the good guys appearing decidedly bland. Although Dracula is accompanied by gratuitous lava red and orange back projections and some almost avant-garde pixilation, really Lee has little to do. But what, you may ask, of the titular corpuscular fluid and its potential culinary properties? Sadly the film was never released in Flavourama but visually it begins akin to red poster paint powder, develops into a crimson bubbling froth and ends up with unrivalled depth of body and achingly intense scarlet highlights. Viscosity high. Realism low. Wonderfully camp, gothic and occasionally gory.

87min, 15, Warner Home Video, Fang Factor Three and a dribble.

Scars Of Dracula (1970)

Dir: Roy Ward Baker

St: Dennis Waterman, Christopher Lee, Patrick Troughton

Puzzlingly it seems that Dracula can be reanimated by bat puppets vomiting pillar box red non-drip gloss paint on his ashes. The Dulux-enhanced Count lurks in his castle. In the neighbouring village, Matthew is in trouble with the girls again, causing him to hotfoot from domestic hassles. But before you can say 'nosferatu' he's whisked off in a mist-clogged coach for a meeting at Drac's residence, fends off the rapacious Tanya and is then dispatched. His brother Simon and girlfriend Sarah try to search for him and you can guess where they end up looking...

By the late 60s the halcyon days of Hammer were over. Unable to compete with the rising relaxation in censorship and burdened, it seemed, with the ability to create only period horror tales, the company began to flounder. *Scars Of Dracula* saw them move into more violent territory with the remarkably gory opening massacre at the church setting the tone for much of the decade to come. Today though this just highlights the camp appeal of the film as the effects are so overblown and the histrionics of the cast most amusing. Chief joy comes from Dennis Waterman in pre-*Sweeney* and *Minder* days wearing ill-fitting hose and talking with the squeakiest public school accent imaginable. Christopher Lee's contact lenses now make him look like he's had a heavy drinking session the night before, but despite this he's still a commanding figure. Not that it's all bad, the scene where Waterman has to escape from a mountaintop castle's window features a great forced perspective glass painting, even if the whole effect is pinched from *Black Narcissus*.

91min, 18, Warner Home Video, Fang Factor Two.

Dracula AD 1972 (er, 1972)

Dir: Alan Gibson

St: Christopher Lee, Peter Cushing, Stephanie Beacham

The ludicrously monikered Johnny Alucard and his gang of ageing 'yoofs' raise the Count in a disused London church. Not that such necromantic activity gets in the way of their incessant frugging and outrageous bell-bottoms. One of these is Jessica Van Helsing, relation of...we think you know by now, and the Count wants her. Turning Alucard he demands to make Jessica his bride.

Hammer meets *Hair* in this atrociously misguided attempt to create a hip-cat-Count. Bland direction does little to divert the mind from the appalling script and gratuitous fashion. Even the puns are woefully pre-modern. That said we do get to see Christopher Neame take a shower when he's a vampire, with hilarious results. Watch only if you like laughing at other people's misfortune.

95min, 18, Warner Home Video, Fang Factor One Baby.

The Satanic Rites Of Dracula (1973)

Dir: Alan Gibson
St: Christopher Lee, Peter Cushing, Joanna Lumley

A rather ineffectual Civil Service agent escapes from Pelham House with tales of Satanic rituals attended by the country's most powerful men. Worse still there are a multitude of hippie snipers silencing anyone who gets in the way. Better call Van Helsing and his intelligent but patronised granddaughter Jessica to help a clandestine investigation. They uncover a conspiracy to unleash a hyper-virulent form of the bubonic plague. Only one mind could be behind such a diabolically fiendish plan, Count Dracula. But surely he died two years ago? Well, as chance would have it the Denham conglomerate have pitched their multinational business on the site of Dracula's last resting place and Mr Denham is not famous for his daytime charity work.

Dracula is dead and well and living in London (as one print was called) – temporarily, for this is the last of Hammer's Dracula films. It's a pity really as, while this contains some nice ideas and the odd interesting sequence (the brides dying in a sprinkler haze is incongruous but looks great and Dracula's final demise is heavily signposted but nonetheless different) it lacks sustaining power. After we've visited the Baptism of Blood in flashback for the fifth time it does get a little tiresome. The premise that Dracula may well be fed up of all this resurrection lark and just wants peace is a well used one but the bubonic plague twist is suitably operatic. Shame that it's so virulent it wouldn't get the opportunity to spread, and with rotting flesh side-effects it's unlikely anyone would want to get too near anyway!

84min, 18, Warner Home Video, Fang Factor Two.

There were 3 films made by Hammer based on the Le Fanu story *Carmilla*, which became known as the Karnstein trilogy.

The Vampire Lovers (1970)

Dir: Roy Ward Baker
St: Ingrid Pitt, Madeleine Smith, Peter Cushing

Baron Hartog avenges the death of his sister by killing the undead Karnsteins in the province of Styria. But he overlooks Mircalla, who reappears years later at the home of the General and his daughter Laura. Laura is seduced by Mircalla, under the eyes of her own fiancé Carl and eventually dies. Mircalla moves to the home of Morton and his daughter Emma (can you spot the trend yet?) seducing the girl, butler Renton and her governess, whilst also taking care of the savvy doctor who tries to deck the halls with boughs of garlic (tra-la-la-la-la). The only way to stop the salacious siren is by the timeous teaming of Morton, Carl and the 'bloody' Baron.

Screenplay writer Tudor Gates' original intention for *The Vampire Lovers* was to test the limits of the BBFC's acceptance of sexually explicit material - the state censors still had a script approval stage at this time and it was felt that period pieces or fantasy films could be more explicit due to their detachment from day-to-day living. Because this was a potentially risky venture, Hammer spread the cost of production with AIP, American drive-in exploitation film specialists. They need not have concerned themselves, the film is as British as afternoon tea and nearly as prudish. That Ingrid Pitt is decapitated has been seen by some writers as punishment for her lesbianism but really it is no different to the fate of any screen vampire - they are punished for the threat that they pose to 'decent' society, regardless of sexual orientation. The dreamlike sequences of mist-clad graveyards are evocative and atmospheric, a point emphasised by eerie use of sound, but sit uneasily with the 'BBC Jane Austin adaptation' sequences that bind the minimal plot together. Cushing is as deadly serious as ever, Pitt adds kitsch charm and dear Madeleine Smith maintains an endearingly doe-eyed innocence - as though she has inadvertently stumbled in from a parlour vignette. Over-hyped on release, the film was successful enough to spawn two sequels.

90min, 15, Rank Video, Fang Factor Two.

Lust For A Vampire (1970)

Dir: Jimmy Sangster
St: Ralph Bates, Barbara Jefford, Susan Leigh

An innocent serving wench has her throat slit to resurrect the delectable Mircalla, who takes residence in a finishing school under the shadow of her ancestral castle. Visiting pervert writer Lestrange deceives his way into an English teacher's position at the school so that he can ogle the lasses. He lodges with Giles, a history teacher with unusual extra-curricula research traits. Soon everyone is falling for Mircalla's charms and local girls go missing. Lestrange uses the most outrageous chat up lines to indulge in some (Le)strange love with Mircalla, but his infatuation can't prevent the rise of peasant power to overthrow the Karnstein curse.

Sangster takes directorial duties for the weakest but most entertaining of the Karnstein trilogy. Bates stars but gets nowhere near the final reel - his character fluctuating wildly from Will Hay schoolmaster to slobbering "servant of the devil," reversing his cross and prostrating himself before Mircalla. He is not alone - all men desire her and so does any woman under thirty with nice breasts (bit convenient that). When Lestrange finally gets to make love (although he remains suspiciously well adorned) we are 'treated' to a playing of the (s)hit single *Strange Love* which further drags the film towards cult turkey status. Stretching credulity to the maximum, the girls wonder why Giles stares at them - this is when they wander around in see-through night-clothes and perform 'Greco/Roman' dancing that looks like synchronised swimming without the water! All the villagers are suitably twitchy - "Burn down the castle!" they yell at any opportunity. The opening is fairly effective as we see a veiled skeleton slowly turn into the blood-drenched Mircalla and there's a lovely shot of a body being dumped into a dried out well, but ultimately this is one to watch for the cheese factor.

91min, 18, Warner Home Video, Fang Factor Two.

Twins Of Evil (1971)

Dir: John Hough
St: Peter Cushing, Madeleine and Mary Collinson

Twins Maria and Frieda have come to stay with Uncle Gustav and Aunt Kathy. Gustav is head of a group of religious fanatics who burn accused witches, but can't quite work up the nerve to eliminate the promiscuous but powerful Count Karnstein. Karnstein is getting tired of his pagan set-pieces so the timely entrance of his long-dead relative Mircalla livens matters up - inviting the mischievous Frieda over he turns her. Uncle Gustav happens upon a feeding Frieda in the forest and locks up this "twin of evil," but Karnstein does the switcheroony routine with goody-two-shoes Maria. By the time everyone figures out what's happening, the vamps have regrouped for a final showdown.

Surprisingly this remains not only the best of the Karnstein trilogy but also one of Hammer's most thought-provoking and socially critical films. It does still provide the bodice-ripping and bloodletting we've come to know and love, but there's a message too. Often the vampire hunter is the dullest character in a film but Cushing gives his all as the grotesquely misguided Uncle Gustav. The Brotherhood are a fanatical religious group of men who use the *Bible* as a means of justifying the torture and murder of young girls. Their Puritanism is sexual - "After more girls to burn?" mocks the Count, caught in flagrante by Gustav's gang. Karnstein may be evil but at least he knows it. The edge of Gustav's gleeful adoption of capital punishment makes for far more uneasy viewing than the Count's supernatural dalliances, perhaps because Gustav is a believable evil while Karnstein is a decadent fantasy bogeyman. Regardless, *Twins Of Evil* is the unexpected high note of the series, a lean enjoyable romp with a plea for tolerance.

83min, 18, Cinema Club, Fang Factor Three and half a twin.

And there's more...

Brides Of Dracula (1960)

Dir: Terence Fisher
St: Peter Cushing
Abandoned, Marianne Danielle is taken in by Baroness Meinster. Spotting the Baroness' son, chained like an animal but completely rational, she releases him. Later, seeing the drained corpse of the Baroness, Marianne flees but the Baron is abroad and his slaughtered brides return from the grave to terrorise the living. Only Van Helsing can save the day.

Brides remains an unusual addition to the genre. Part thriller with an outrageously Oedipal subtext and part swashbuckling gung-ho action, the sudden change of pace makes for an exhilarating climax to a good idea that was basically running out of steam. The initial premise of a handsome aristocratic prisoner chained by a cackling hag twists character and audience expectations on their heads when it's revealed that the Baron is a vampire. The languid pace of these revelations creates a sense of Grimm, folk tale escalation. When all is revealed and Van Helsing is on the trail, events gallop away - Cushing has never been more dramatic. Whatever the ludicrous premise of the windmill-bound conclusion, it is undeniably energetic and exciting. See Van Helsing poisoned by the vampire's penetrating kiss! See him cauterise the wound with a brand! Wince as holy water bubbles on the Baron's face! Gasp at Van Helsing leaping at the deadly flapping windmill sails! Cracking stuff, beguiling plot, luscious brides - classy fantasy.

Fang Factor Three.

Kiss Of The Vampire (1962)

Dir: Don Sharp
St: Clifford Evans, Edward De Souza, Jennifer Daniel

Newlyweds Gerald and Marianne, stranded and out of petrol, seek refuge at a local hotel. They are delighted to receive an invitation to dine at Dr Ravner's sumptuous home and meet his charming family. But why does the innkeeper's wife cry all the time, and why is batty Professor Zemmer always drunk? When Marianne disappears after a party and everyone denies her existence, Gerald must find help. But to whom can he turn?

From Zemmer 'staking' a coffin with a shovel, a groan reverberating and blood oozing through, it is clear that Hammer (still in the early days of its horror output) were becoming more daring. Indeed, the couple are now allowed to at least kiss before being interrupted for tea. The society Ravner shows the outside world is a wholesome 'family,' hiding the vampire cult within, his children thoroughly hospitable, although there is one sister who seems to slink about the house. She is Tanya, one of cinema's most alluring vampires, the very picture of innocence - eager to find and befriend the newly turned, distraught when she discovers Zemmer's actions. Deep down though, she's wicked and deceitful, her eyes light up with terrible anticipation when offered Giles as her consort. The final denouement's astonishing depiction of thousands upon thousands of bats destroying the cult is another masterpiece of effects work. This is one of Hammer's rarest films, the one that got away, but do try to get a copy, it's well worth it.

Fang Factor Four.

Countess Dracula (1970)

Dir: Peter Sasdy
St: Ingrid Pitt, Nigel Green

Her husband dead and with the estate split between herself and daughter Elona, Countess Elizabeth also has to contend with ageing wrinkles and a poor complexion. A chance discovery whilst beating her servant, reveals that blood does more wonders for the skin than Oil of Ulay, so she instigates a strictly sticky bathing policy, has her daughter kidnapped by a mute Mongol with limited culinary skills and poses as the now rapacious Elona. Longtime lover Dobi helps out, but the rejuvenated Countess now seeks younger flesh in the shape of Imran, whom she plans to marry. The effects of the blood last shorter periods and with the revelation that only virgins can supply Elizabeth's unusual beauty treatment, it gets increasingly difficult to hide the bodies as the wedding day approaches.

Once notorious for the publicity shot of Ingrid Pitt climbing naked out of a bath of virgin's blood, *Countess Dracula* has all the ingredients for either a serious or exploitative film, or both (see Borowczyk's *Immoral Tales* with Paloma Picasso in the Elizabeth Bathory role). Sadly, appallingly leaden direction, insipid cinematography, average score, plodding script and bad pacing conspire to make this a deeply dull experience. Even the sumptuous wardrobe is offset by laughable beards. How Sasdy can take such an eminently filmable tale and turn it into 90 minutes of tedium is a mystery. Despite a spirited performance, Ingrid Pitt spends most of the film either pouting or looking distraught because her face is covered in flesh-coloured plasticine. Too literary in intent but not in quality, it lacks in suspense and, crucially, is devoid of all but a modicum of gratuitous sex and violence to compensate. One of those films you watch time and again, hoping that you were mistaken as to its quality. You weren't.

89min, 18, Video Collection, Fang Factor One.

Vampire Circus (1971)

Dir: Robert Young
St: Adrienne Corri, Laurence Payne, Lalla Ward, Dave Prowse

Count Mitterhaus likes nothing better than to dine on small children and roll around naked with the Burgermeister's wife. He is therefore somewhat perturbed when the townsfolk decide to interrupt his frolickings, torch his pad and ram a hunk of wood in his chest. He vows death to the children. Years pass and life in Schtettel is not good as the plague is taking its toll. What they need is a bit of cheering up which is why the appearance of The Circus Of Nights is most welcome. However all is not what it seems and the children soon start disappearing.

With a budget small even by Hammer standards, a tight shooting schedule and loopy plot, *Vampire Circus* doesn't seem to promise a great deal. But before the opening credits are over you know you are in for a treat. Young keeps everything moving at a cracking pace mixing a potent cocktail of sex, violence and surreal imagery. There are boy and girl vampire twins who seduce young children through mirrors and have a close empathetic link. There is Emil, Romany panther lycanthrope with a sideline in seducing the Burgermeister's daughter. Or how about barrel organ playing silent strongman (in pre-Green Cross Man days) David Prowse? Or the dwarf? The scary chimps? There's a cavern full of bats and chained up decomposing corpses, a catchy steam organ soundtrack, shock body discoveries and the wanton slaughter of yuppie students. All of this is made even more appealing by the audacious use of in-camera special effects and careful editing. The Hall of Mirrors is shot like Cocteau and the acrobats changing into animals mid-air is breathtaking in its simplicity. The circus performers slink around like the animals they portray and ooze sexual promise. There are too many enjoyable moments to mention, the only blemish on an otherwise squeaky clean slate is Count Mitterhaus himself - the supposedly irresistible aristocrat is horribly unkind on the eye, but he's not in it for long and gets a highly entertaining death scene. A-grade entertainment but don't pack your brain.

83min, 18, Cinema Club, Fang Factor Four (sorry Count, you're too ugly for a five).

Captain Kronos, Vampire Hunter (1972)

Dir: Brian Clemens

St: Horst Janson, Caroline Munroe

Cap'n Kronos, dashing sword-swinging vampire hunter, travels with his hunchbacked friend Grost - "What he doesn't know about vampires wouldn't fill a flea's codpiece." This is fortunate as they are going to need every trick in the book to free Durward from its curse. Local youthful girls are being found drained of age but who is responsible? Is it hereditary combo Paul and Sarah, whose close-cropped dyed hair was all the rage in the Eighteenth century? Is it mild-mannered Dr Marcus, who invited the hunters over, perhaps in a double bluff manoeuvre? Or the wizened bedridden widow, who couldn't be related to the Karnsteins, oh no?

Brimming with clever ideas and bizarre touches *Captain Kronos* bears all the hallmarks of Clemens' (who also wrote and produced) remarkable work on *The Avengers* - outré characterisation, accentuated deep focus camerawork and ridiculously convoluted plotting. When Dr Marcus realises he has become a vampire he implores the duo kill him. Ornate stake through the heart? Nope. Hanging in a chair tied up? Nope. Impaled on a steel crucifix? Ah, at last. So Grost forges a sword out of a huge crucifix to fight the vampires, Kronos having first disarmed the misguided villagers who think he is a murdering psychopath. It comes as some surprise then that this is all so unremittingly dull. Caroline Munroe's Garla saved from the stocks at the film's opening just hangs around, looking sultry and providing the good Cap'n with some hay rolling relief, only to be discarded at the end. Grost, a potentially interesting character, gets two lines of introspection about his appearance while Kronos himself is too busy playing the swashbuckling hero to provoke sympathy, his ruffled shirt and hairy chest are particularly off-putting. The intention for the film to be the precursor for a television franchise is all too evident, despite its taut running time you get the feeling this is a 50-minute TV show dragged to barely feature length. A wasted opportunity.

82min, 15, Fang Factor Two.

The Legend Of The Seven Golden Vampires (1974)

Dir: Roy Ward Barker
St: Peter Cushing, David Chiang

Count Dracula travels to China where, as luck would have it, Van Helsing is on a lecture tour, telling academics of brave Hsi Tien-En and his victory over one of the Seven Golden Vampires by the power of Buddha. Van Helsing fears that the village of Ping Kuei is still under the terror of the remaining six and launches an expedition, protected by the Hsi brothers and sister Mai Kwei. Sometimes the power of evil needs to be overthrown by the co-operation of many.

East meets West in this bizarre Hammer/Shaw Brothers crossover designed to stave off the financial pressures of both companies by producing a hybrid kung-fu/vampire film. Unfortunately director Barker's inexperience regarding Hong Kong filming practices (they are shot silent - the first sound sync rushes returned with jet-plane noises, not really appropriate for a period film) resulted in a rushed production that didn't fully exploit the talented cast. Matters were not helped by a truly warped script. It's all jolly good fun to watch though and never flags as you are assaulted with a barrage of occasionally breathtaking images. The shambling armies of the dead, commanded by the mounted golden vampires, with their peasant weapons make for an unforgettable sight. Every method of mass staking is employed including a tragic moment when Ching holds Vanessa, the woman he now loves and impales them both due to her vampirism. Admittedly Cushing looks bemused a great deal of the time, but this is a great, messy, exciting romp which never allows coherence to interfere with a bloody good ruck.

88min, 18, Warner Home Video, Fang Factor Three.

4. European Delicacies

European cinema has traditionally been viewed as racier than its Hollywood cousin, more liberal and laid-back. Part of the forming of the MPAA was in response to 'art' films becoming acceptable fodder for both the intelligentsia and the raincoat brigade. There needed to be a clearer distinction between art and smut. The vampire films of the late 60s and early 70s are often associated with the dodgy end of the spectrum but really they have their roots in the freethinking liberal art movements of Europe rather than the grindhouse sensibilities of the American exploitation circuit. At least until their downfall. Roger Vadim first scandalised America with his film *And God Created Woman* which projected Brigitte Bardot onto the international scene. The rest of his life was spent trying to relive that cause célèbre. In 1960 he set the foundations, albeit coyly, for the resurgence in the lesbian vampire film with *Blood And Roses*. A lyrical art film based on Le Fanu's *Carmilla* and featuring a particularly touching end where the main vampire is eviscerated on barbed wire. This was not the only influence that Italian cinema had on the genre. The early 60s were a period of frenetic activity in the film industry. Mario Bava's *Mask Of Satan* (1961) features genre icon Barbara Steele as a vengeful witch, back from the grave, seeking the blood of the kindred of her tormentors. *L'Horrible Secreto del Dr Hitchcock* (dir Freda, 1963) is a Sadean tale of necrophilia and unnatural love that replaces *Mask Of Satan's* stark black and white photography with lurid pulp colour. Meanwhile Spanish director Jesus Franco began churning out a phenomenal number of pictures, many involving sex, torture and bloodlust. These films paved the way for the vampire's heyday, a few brief years that would see the emergence of Jean Rollin, the king of the vampire film and, in Belgium, the creation of the finest vampire movie ever made.

Daughters Of Darkness (Le Rouge Aux Lèvres) (1970, Belgium)

Dir: Harry Kumel

St: Delphine Seyrig, Andrea Rau, Danielle Ouimet, John Karlen

Stefan and Valerie are on honeymoon, having secretly married, and are off to England to break the news to Stefan's domineering 'mother.' However they find themselves staying more than one night at the Grand Hotel Des Hermes, a near deserted opulent art deco oasis in the coastal town of Ostende, where the only other guests are Countess Elizabeth and her beautiful companion Ilona. The young couple get slowly embroiled in the Countess' hypnotic, loving world of decadence and gentle persuasion but their own relationship deteriorates as a result. Stefan is not all he seems, compelled to watch the bodies of a spate of murder victims that have plagued the town and instigating an affair with Ilona that culminates in shower-drenched death. Clearly he has to go and moreover the Countess requires a new companion to accompany her on long sensual nights.

Let us not mince words - *Daughters Of Darkness* is without a doubt the most wonderful vampire film ever made and Countess Elizabeth its most beguiling, alluring vampire. Seyrig (of *Last Year In Marienbad* fame) gives such a compelling, lover's whisper of a performance you cannot fail to be captivated by her need to be loved, all enhanced by the astonishing wardrobe of glittered dresses that must have eaten up a substantial portion of the film's budget. If Ilona is more conventionally beautiful, her performance is no less remarkable. The fear in her eyes as Stefan drags her towards the shower or the wretched vomitings following feeding, compound her strange relationship with the Countess. No one is who they seem - Stefan is a repressed homosexual and even Valerie hides her yearnings for female companionship. Kumel's film is drenched in resplendent colour, a decadent, lyrical tour de force of aesthetic decadence, no shot is wasted. The script is so tight that the ostensibly simple fable-like plot reveals more subtle nuances on each subsequent viewing. Despite acknowledging the bloody aspects of vampirism, *Daughters Of Darkness* is not a horror film. Kumel is more concerned with the sensuality and allure of the vampire, the ageless beauty than the process of immortality. More is made of Elizabeth's bat-like cape back-lit at dusk than the mechanics of the feed. That it ends in part tragedy makes it a weepy too, so there's something for everyone. A magical visual and intellectual feast that is without peer. Sensual, shocking and beautiful. Perfect.

96min, 18, Tartan Video, Fang Factor Six.

Vampiros Lesbos (Die Erbin Des Dracula) (1970, Germany/Spain)

Dir: Jesus Franco

St: Soledad Miranda, Dennis Price

Linda feels the calling of Countess Carody - a performer in Pygmalion-style lesbian stage shows, a dream or a client? Her psychiatrist thinks she just needs a better lover than Omar. She takes a job to oversee the Countess' will, aware of her unusual connection to the Draculas. Before long she is carried comatose to a bedroom by the curiously named Morpho and visited by the delectable Countess.

With *Vampiros Lesbos* Franco is in familiar stylistic territory - the use of repetitive score, the fetishism, the longing of eternal love denied and the essential erotic stage show sequences. Sultry Soledad Miranda starred in 8 of Franco's oeuvre before tragically dying in a car accident - her role sizzles with sexuality. Unlike some of Franco's output, the tight budget actually improves the film by forcing an insular perspective on proceedings and relying upon instinct to realise his vision. Style is something *Vampiros Lesbos* has in spades. From the outset the viewer is assaulted by outrageously wide lenses shooting garishly lit abstractions of sexual violence, with mood-enhancing scorpions and insects edited in to give a detachment from reality. The normally present jazz soundtrack is replaced by a psychedelic whirl of Hammond organs and sitars to evoke an other-worldly hallucinogenic quality. Intoxicating.

85min, 18, Redemption, Fang Factor Four.

Bram Stoker's Count Dracula (aka El Conde Dracula) (1971, Spain/Germany/Italy)

Dir: Jes(u)s Franco

St: Herbert Lom, Christopher Lee, Klaus Kinski, Soledad Miranda

Transylvania. Train. Jonathan. Castle. Dracula. Brides. Coffin. Escape. London. Lucy. Bites. Dead. Undead. Dead. Renfield. Flies. Castle. Coffin. Burnt. End.

For as long as anyone can remember Christopher Lee has stated his intent to play Dracula by the book so the opportunity to be in a film "exactly as he [Stoker] wrote" must have seemed like a good one. It wasn't. By this time Lee had already worked for Franco a number of times, notably on some quickie Fu Manchu films, so perhaps he should have known what he was letting himself in for. The tired and generally unsubstantiated accusations of Franco's excesses in the camera department probably have their genesis in this film – it's all over the place, panning and zooming about like a home video nightmare. Kinski spends a great deal of the film in a straightjacket, presumably to prevent him running off set and Lom's performance as Jonathon is nearly as poor as Franco's own atrocious cameo. Only Lee and Miranda seem to be making any effort at all but she is hampered by poor make-up and he by a dazzling array of appalling false moustaches. If you have the stamina you might just get as far as the menacing stuffed ferret and giraffe scene by which point you'll be either comatose or in stitches. Completely devoid of tension or artistic merit there is no reason to watch this at all. A 'Towers of London' production (after producer Harry Towers) that should be locked up.

96min, 12, 4-Front, Fang Factor One.

The Curse Of The Vampyr (1971, Spain)

Dir: Joseph de Lacy
St: Beatriz Lacy, Diana Sorrel, Loretta Martin

Carl von Rysselbert invites Dr Metterlick and her glamorous assistant Erika to look after his father, the Baron, and help destroy the superstitions of the local townspeople. Years before they had staked the delectable Margaret, but a reversal of the staking process brings her back to enjoy naked lesbian romps with nibbles to go. Even Carl sports a fine set of fangs ready to sink into all and sundry. What will end the madness of the full moon disease?

From the opening staking in extreme wide angle and Joseph Larn's almost Eastern European soundtrack you know you are in for a tacky treat. Director de Lacy (Jose Maria Elorietta) keeps things well paced with some moody atmospherics and surprisingly effective lighting. Even if the plot lurches into unfathomable surrealism at times this merely adds to its camp charm - it even includes some mad hippies on Raleigh chopper bikes! All the vampiric elements are correct and present: ominous warnings, swirly dramatic capes, candles and some surprisingly impressive teeth. The soft core fumblings are as erotic as the flu, but somehow this makes the suggestive scenes far more sensual. Enjoyable, unashamedly low-budget, mild Eurosleaze of the sort that restores your faith in exploitation film-making. But wait! "Erika! Don't go in there, the lake's full of quicksand!"

85min, 18, Cinema Club, Fang Factor Three.

Female Vampire (aka The Bare Breasted Countess, Erotikill) (1973, France/Belgium)

Dir: Jesus Franco (as J P Johnson)

St: Lina Romay, Jack Taylor, Alice Arno, Jess Franck (guess who)

The mute aristocrat Countess Irina Karlstein wanders, near naked, up to a fashion victim farmhand and fellates him to death on the chicken wire. The poultry are not impressed. The poor girl - she just wants "an end to this bloody race...the curse of the Karlsteins" but can't help draining the bodily fluids of anyone in her way, including Anna, an unsympathetic psychiatrist and a bad judge of acceptable footwear. Even her own bed is not safe from her rapacious sexual appetite. But don't get unduly concerned - Dr Roberts and Dr Orloff are on hand to talk garbled nonsense at each other and find a solution.

No matter how fetishistic or deranged, the allure of the vampire film is its implication, sensuality and embracing of the forbidden. With the sudden worldwide explosion in hard-core pornography, the vampire film lost its edge and became a quaint reminder of the past. *Female Vampire* marks the end of an era. Despite the obvious charms of Ms Romay (Franco's beau at the time) there is no suggestion or anticipation to entice the viewer into the film - the titles have not even finished before we've had ample opportunity to view her, wandering around clad only in boots, cloak and belt. There is a sense that perhaps Franco is concerned with questions of loneliness, longing and the pitfalls of immortality - the repetition of the feed, the sexual nature of devouring, the pain in love. However one more turgid bout of pornographic couplings later and you're left in no doubt that this is merely squalid, depressing and unforgivably dull. The out-of-focus pubic zooms are embarrassingly juvenile and the lighting does little justice to anyone. Censored by over 6 minutes, courtesy of the BBFC, you can't help wishing that they'd snipped a further 92 and saved everyone the bother.

92min, 18, Redemption, Fang Factor One.

Vampyres (1974, UK)

Dir: Jose Larraz

St: Marianne Morris, Anulka

Fran and Miriam lounge around their impressive house and spend the days in the company of their excellent collection of vintage wines. Food is reasonable - pick up a dumb bloke by hitch-hiking, take him home, butter him up a bit and drink his blood. Later they can dump the body in his own car. It's all going swimmingly until Fran becomes a little overattached to Ted, keeping him like a living larder.

The power in *Vampyres* lies in the utmost simplicity of the plot - the story just unfolds like an adult parable. Larraz, shooting in England for the first time, almost manages to pull off some Rollinesque imagery as the cloaked girls wander through the woods and graveyard, but it lacks the ethereal innocence of Rollin's work. Still he does manage to make a surprisingly atmospheric job of lighting the house, particularly the cellar when the two kill off an odious wine snob. Fran and Miriam make a charming couple and are extremely accommodating hostesses. It's just the company they choose to keep that lets them down. The lack of explanation, the beguiling pre-credit sequence and the subtle conclusion do a lot to offset the clearly limited budget and Ted's revolting tongue work. Put it away mate!

81min, 18, MIA, Fang Factor Two and a lick.

Nosferatu The Vampyre (1979, Germany/France)

Dir: Werner Herzog

St: Klaus Kinski, Isabelle Adjani, Bruno Ganz

Dracula needs a new place to camp out and where better than the disused apartment just opposite Jonathon and Lucy's? He may as well bring along a few rodent friends and the plague so they can all join in the party. Jonathon may not like his new neighbour's amorous intentions towards his fiancée but hey, he's in no fit state to argue - he's as lively as a rock and has a strange aversion to crumbled communion wafers…

Warner Herzog was one of the many star auteurs of New German Cinema. A towering madman who would drag his cast through jungles and over mountains to realise his grandiose visions. His love/hate relationship with Kinski produced some of that movement's most astonishing films. *Nosferatu* is not one of them. Herzog's version of Murnau's classic is concerned with decay and the prolonged agonies of suffering. Something that is drummed home in every shot and wretched line. Rather than being "as profound as a thousand nights," the film is soporific enlivened only by some monumentally pretentious and unintentionally hilarious dialogue. Kinski looks like Gary Numan in a beanie, turning Max Schreck's outstandingly creepy performance into one that lurches from horror to stupidity. Herzog's inspiration for the camerawork seems to be from Franco's miserable *El Conde Dracula* although to be fair the painterly use of light in some murky interiors do recall the Grand Masters. Matters are not improved by a ghastly, morbid requiem accompanying even a pleasant walk in the mountains. However, full credit must be paid to the charming rats that litter the coffins and plague scenes - they are so adorable and fluffy you want to cuddle every one of them, probably not the reaction Herzog had in mind. A waste of talent all around, Adjani just has to stand or lie about in corpse-like despair and the great Bruno Ganz is treated badly throughout, suffering the indignity of a heavily signposted 'shock' ending. Unforgivably ponderous, pompous and dismal. By the time you reach the startling shot of a dead horse in the market square you have the distinct impression that Herzog has been flogging it. Kinski returned, with hair, in *Vampire In Venice* (1988).

96min, 15, Guild, Fang Factor One.

5. Only Partly Reality

Jean Rollin's persistence has made him the world's premier producer of vampire films over the last 35 years, yet many people have not heard of him and some of those that have wish they hadn't! Rollin's world is not the world of action, dynamics and quick cutting - it is slow, languid and mood drenched. His detractors point to dull, plotless non-narratives with naked people talking gibberish, pointless focus on ornaments and too many beaches. His admirers appreciate the visual poetry, the expressive use of light and form, the bravura lack of concern for bland linear narrative structures and the total cinematic experience rendered on horrendously small budgets.

Such an intense style is not generated in a vacuum. Visually he derives his composition and set decoration from 3 main sources - the surrealists, pulp serials and the underground comic fraternity. His visual flair reflects works by painters such as Delvaux and the collages of Clovis Trouille. Much of his cinematic style derives from Feuillade's *Les Vampires*, sharing the same love of pulpy crime novels. From the world of comics stems his compositional style and occasionally kinetic camera movements, blending the erotic images of underground illustrators from the 50s with the thriving enthusiasm of 60s fetish culture.

Rollin's first short *Les Amours Jaunes* (1958) was made when the director was just 20. His debut feature *Le Viol Du Vampire* (1967) was a welcome but unexpected scandal on its release and Rollin followed this up with a succession of further vampire projects. *La Rose De Fer* (1973) was a departure. It was a surreal tale of two people lost and scared, overlooked by a cold landscape and the chill of stone. However his loyal following hated the film's lack of blood, sex and vampires. He returned with *Les Démoniaques* (1974) but by then, despite the beauty of *La Rose De Fer*, the damage was done. Additionally the film world had moved on. Low budgets now meant only one thing, pornography. Whilst his films were certainly provocative and sensual (many of his films remain heavily censored in the UK) they were never pornographic. From now on Rollin would produce his films, his way, when he could afford to, and in between he worked on a number of pornos to make ends meet, using the pseudonym Michel Gentil.

Rollin's most recent vampire tale is *Les Deux Orphelines Vampires* (1995), a wry twist on the popularist 19th century book *Les Deux Orphelines,* which Rollin adapted from his own novel. A resurgence in the vampire genre has led to the rediscovery of his remarkable and idiosyncratic oeuvre which is something to rejoice.

Le Viol Du Vampire (The Rape Of The Vampire) (1967)

Dir: Jean Rollin
St: Solange Pradel, Bernard Letrou, Catherine Devil, Jacqueline Sieger
Part One: Four vampire sisters have lived in their château for 2 centuries, surrounded by myth and intolerance. They are wary of strangers, especially ones who purport to cure their affliction.
Part Two: The Queen of the Vampires arrives and is not impressed by the manipulation involved in the case of the 4 sisters. She discovers treachery but still goes ahead with the great Blood Wedding that will see the vampires rise triumphant.
Rollin's first feature is "A melodrama in two parts," a pulp black and white poem of exaggerated expressions and penny dreadful emotions. It was greeted with incredulity by a violent audience at its Paris première during the heady student riots in May 1968 - a period of radical political rethinking that was certainly not ready for Rollin's unique vision. The aftermath of the riots would see fevered output from the nouvelle vague directors, but for Rollin his timeous debut would prove as much a blessing as a curse. All his preoccupations are laid bare: the love of trees, the beach, châteaux, naked women, flagellation and of course vampires. Filmed in a poetic style that recalls Cocteau or the early expressionists and surrealists, *Viol* mocks the viewer with half-grasped narrative turns and fragmented ideas. Characters die, relive, die again, there are two duels, guns blaze, the

camera whirls in Gothic splendour. The effect on the viewer is either instant adoration or condemnation. Chief figure is the Amazonian Queen of Vampires, a magisterial figure of art deco dominance. That many of these ideas would crop up in later films is not just the sign of an auteur, it is a necessity - there are too many for just one film. With Felliniesque parades and theatre, medical experiments, Sax Rohmer-style devious tortures and blind beach skittles, *Viol* paved the way for all Rollin's subsequent work. Dizzying. Intoxicating yet sensual. Dangerous and lyrical.

90min, 18, Redemption, Fang Factor Four.

La Vampire Nue (1969)

Dir: Jean Rollin
St: Oliver Martin, Maurice Lemaitre, Caroline Cartier
Pierre is curious as to what his father does at his mysterious parties. He becomes embroiled in a bizarre blue-hooded suicide cult with exotic rituals involving a captured girl. He's told that she suffers a rare blood disorder that they are trying to research. Regardless, he hatches a plan to free the poor thing, now locked in the dungeon of a country château. But are his father's explanations complete, or are there others of her kind seeking her salvation?

Medical experiments with colour-coded hooded doctors, animal-masked stalkers of a frightened girl, rhythmic dancing, stunning fetish costumes and blazing guns - Rollin goes sci-fi in a wholly unconventional sense. The vampires here are immortals, calm and socially minded, existing in a different dimension and offering hope, not death. Peppered with grotesquely mutilated children's dolls, suspicious serums, animal howlings and baroque locations, Rollin creates a wonderful sense of mystery and revelation. The beautiful symmetries in the cinematography are matched by the structured yet fragile plot. With incredibly fluid tracking, a heightened sense of colour and a varied score, this remains an assured picture that only drags at the moments that probably secured its distribution in the first place! Sumptuous, decadent and bizarre.

88min, 18, Redemption, Fang Factor Four.

Le Frisson Des Vampires (1970)

Dir: Jean Rollin
St: Sandra Julien, Nicole Nancel, Marie-Pierre
Newlyweds Isa and Anthony spend their wedding night at the castle of Isa's cousins, but on arrival are told that they died the previous day.

Looked after by two nubile servants, Isa's grief leads her to reject her husband and she sleeps alone. As the clock strikes midnight she is whisked away to bizarre rituals and given the vampire's kiss. It then comes as quite a shock to find her cousins are working in the library. Their existence is ironic - vampire hunters of the highest calibre turned into the very beasts they sought to destroy, living on the blood of their hypnotised servants to prevent needless slaughter. And Anthony, bemused, his marriage unconsummated, tries to unravel the mysteries and retain his bride.

From the backlit cemetery and the sepia internments Rollin returns, entrancing the viewer. His camera caresses the rocks of the castle, the nooks with their skulls and burnt-out statues, making it the embodiment of a living entity. Anthony never stands a chance - his wife is seduced by a vampire, crawling from the innards of a Grandfather clock. The twin servant girls wander in time, clutching candlesticks and doing their masters' bidding. The two mad cousins speak in puzzles about their origins as bourgeois vampires, subservient to the vampire errant, all to dizzying 360° pans or tightly framed grotesque close-ups. Rollin's use of sound is harsh but impressive - animal screeches and portentous groans accompany the grandiose ceremonies. Even more astonishing is the aggressive soundtrack, performed and occasionally improvised by Acanthus that adds a further edge of unease. Sensual, colourful and smooth - the ideal introduction to his early work. Oh and there's a skull with flaming eyes in a fishbowl - complete with fish! How does he do that?

90min, 18, Redemption, Fang Factor Four.

Requiem For A Vampire (1971)

Dir: Jean Rollin
St: Marie-Pierre Castel, Louise Dhour, Philippe Gaste

Marie and Michelle, dressed as clowns, are on the run. They seek shelter from their pursuers and come across a cemetery and adjacent château. "They are young, they are virgins, they are to perpetuate our race." The castle is the refuge of the last vampire, a mournful figure who resides in his ostentatious mausoleum accompanied by 3 thuggish half-men and 2 decorous aristocratic women. Erica is undergoing the change from human to vampire, a fate that awaits Marie and Michelle. Given the task of supplying food for the photosensitive ones, Michelle acquiesces but naughty Marie makes sure she loses one of the prerequisites for vampirism.

From the opening shot of clowns brandishing a gun through a broken car window you know this is going to be an audacious and pulpy ride.

Rollin has the impertinence to tell his tale almost entirely visually, for the first 40 minutes there are three lines of dialogue and all of them irrelevant. Drops of colour blossom in the brook as the girls wash off their make-up. In the château the girls come across decomposing bodies, half-naked victims and the sumptuously androgynous Erica playing requiem organ music to a congregation of robed skeletons. Despite the lyrical and illogical juxtaposition of shots this is one of Rollin's more coherent narratives, a lament for a dying race. Even before the last vampire has explained the futility of his attempts to propagate his race, we know he is doomed. Locked up with Erica for all eternity he is a monster by nature, amoral and sympathetic - his final incarceration inevitable and strangely moving. To enhance the agelessness, Rollin shoots the château with as much care and attention as he lavishes on his heroines. It lives inexorably linked to its trapped master. Only the comedic chasing of Michelle by a randy Frenchman and the vampires' unconvincing fangs break the magical spell.

76min, 18, Redemption, Fang Factor Four.

Fascination (1979)

Dir: Jean Rollin
St: Franca Mai, Brigitte Lahaie

What could be nicer than a big glass of tasty ox blood down your local abattoir? For Eva and Elizabeth such sanguinal bovine tipples provide an aperitif for a rather more robust little number during a planned 'girls night in' at their château. Mark is a red coated gun-toting scallywag who nips off with his gang's loot, much to their chagrin, and seeks refuge. What follows is a series of cat-and-mouse games where captives become captors and even the savage gang are not immune to the deadly swoosh of Eva's mighty scythe.

"It's all very melodramatic." Well what do you expect if you enter Eva and Elizabeth's world of madness and death? Guns blaze, dapper criminals make off with stolen gold and two innocent women are held captive in their own château. But the two captives are Rollin non-identical twins who have been taking ox blood under the illusion that it prevents anaemia. The scenes in the abattoir are incredible, dressed in identical Edwardian dresses (one white, one jet black) they sup their blood among the carcasses and carnage. When the 2 play games with the scurrilous Mark they taunt him - "I beg you Mr. Bandit don't kill us!" His masculinity is futile to their giggling sexuality. He is far more able to handle their dominatrix friend Helen than cope with their twisted logic. Ultimately it is Mark who sets up

Eva and Elizabeth's downfall though more by luck than design, taking advantage of Eva's advances unaware that Elizabeth has eyes for him as her lover. A fairy tale for adults dripping with decadence, *Fascination* unravels like a little puzzle towards its ceremonious conclusion. Rollin places the film in a half-glimpsed Edwardian setting (1905) where the two girls waltz to a wind-up gramophone - their home a timeless castle. Seeing Eva, half cloaked in black, cutting through the gang that abused her is a difficult image to forget, but even more so as she returns to the fold of her home, mist on the lake, instrument of death in her hands. Less intense than his previous films, it looks forward to a more commercial style but one that does not compromise the integrity of his vision. At times, it is a little unfocused.

78min, 18, Cinema Club, Fang Factor Three.

La Morte Vivante (The Living Dead Girl) (1982)

Dir: Jean Rollin

St: Marina Pierro, Françoise Blanchard

The dumping of toxic waste leads to the revival of Catherine Valmont from her tomb. Helene, Catherine's blood sister from childhood, realises that her friend is alive when she hears the tune from their old musical box over the telephone. On arrival at the château she finds the bodies of Catherine's victims, their throats ripped out to feed her uncontrollable hunger. Helene begins the process of caring for her sister and disposing of the bodies. But will their love be sufficient to keep them both alive?

Rollin's finest film combines the lyrical poetry of his other works with a strong script and exceptional acting. What sets it apart is that there is an almost commercial coherence to the proceedings that resonates throughout the characterisations - you feel for Catherine and her tragic curse, you sympathise with Helene. Naked and gorged with blood, Catherine plays a melancholy tune on her piano, but this is no cheap exploitation, it is the moving attempt of an unnatural creature to grasp any humanity that remains. Marina Pierro's portrayal of the titular character is haunting - a trailing hand on a rocking horse, a desperate glance, tears streaming down her face in remembrance of times past - which makes the exceptionally violent deaths all the more disturbing in their futility. Rollin's effortless mixing of past and present is never confusing and always relevant - his camera slow and restrained. Truly an emotional, sad, beautiful work of rare maturity.

86min, 18, Redemption, Fang Factor Five.

6. Stay Away, The Dead Is Coming

Supernatural happenings and stirrings from beyond the grave have made regular contributions to the wonderful world of Chinese film since its inception. Ghost stories have always been an important part of Chinese folk law so it was inevitable that cinema would turn to these for inspiration. Despite occasional dallies into the world of the vampire, the Chinese hopping vampire film began to emerge as a genre in the 70s partly in response to the Shaw Brothers' *Legend Of The Seven Golden Vampires*. What this did was create an interest in the field to make the Chinese vampire, not normally the most appealing of undead, into a subject worthy of an entertainment film. Indeed the Chinese term is jiangshi dianying or 'corpse film,' the term vampire being coined later.

Many films use the term zombie or vampire interchangeably, but generally the vampire tends to appear as a more singular entity, like its Western counterpart. The key mover in so much of the development of Hong Kong action genres is Samo Hung - who may not be the most successful of Hong Kong star/producer/directors but is certainly one of the most influential. In 1982 he starred in the jet-black horror comedy *The Dead And The Deadly* (directed by Wu Ma), a macabre tale about marital infidelity, inheritance and greed. Our hapless hero Zhu (Hung) ends up fighting for his life and afterlife when a devious con-trick gets out of hand. With a droll and sudden ending *The Dead And The Deadly* works like an insular cousin for the earlier, more ambitious, though less tightly structured, *Close Encounters Of The Spooky Kind* (Samo Hung 1980). In this film Hung plays Brave Cheung, an amiable buffoon who is always at the receiving end of dodgy gambling games and blunt objects. He is egged on to spend nights in haunted houses, mostly inhabited by his money pinching friends with their ghoulish special effects. But all too soon the spirits are no longer fake and he is in need of some serious spell work and an unfeasibly high altar. One key sequence sees Hung spend the night in the company of a recently deceased, inanimate corpse. It doesn't stay that way - folk lore dictates that should a black cat jump over a dead body then the spirit will become restless and the corpse a vampire! One pussy leap later and Samo's quiet night is seriously disturbed by the relentless, bloodthirsty, hopping menace. Much remarkable kung-fu mayhem ensues, and a lot of it looks very painful! The success of the film left a slew of horror comedies in its wake, but yet again Samo was ahead of the game - for his production company BoHo Films, he negotiated a relatively large budget for what would become the quintessential hopping vampire film - *Mr Vampire*. The film's unqualified artistic and critical success led to numerous sequels and rip-offs. There is *The Ultimate Vampire*, *Vampire Vs Vampire*, *Mr Vampire III, IV, V, VI* (aka *Magic Cop* - a modern day tale of traditional ghostbusting in bustling Hong Kong with Michenko as a gorgeously gowned Japanese ghost and Lam Ching Ying as a spell casting cop), *New Mr Vampire* (aka *Kung Fu Vampire Buster), Toothless Vampires* and so on. There's even a Western version of the hopping genre called *The Jitters*. Vampires also crop up in the sidelines of other, more fantasy-based productions such as Ching Siu-Tung's visually inventive *A Chinese Ghost Story* trilogy. Now a staple of Hong Kong cinema, we can look forward to many more happy hopping years.

Mr Vampire (1985)

Dir: Lau Kun Wai
St: Lam Ching Ying, Moon Lee

Kau is left with his two useless assistants to mind the mortuary business while the boss is out giving the corpses a stroll in the countryside. In three days time they need to rebury Mr Yam because of bad internment information given to him by a fortune-teller he ripped off. As a result, the corpse needs to be securely held at the mortuary. But it bursts free and terrorises the community, leaving granddaughter Yam Ting-Ting fatherless. Poor Ting-Ting. If losing a relative isn't enough, her departed grandfather is proving even more deadly and elusive, while every young chap in the neighbourhood has fallen for her charms, including the young unhinged police officer who is handling the murder. Badly. Not that things are going too well for Kau either. Following a spell in gaol, he is left with one assistant slowly turning into a vampire and the other hopelessly devoted to a demon lover with electric hair and a detachable head.

A milestone in Hong Kong cinema *Mr Vampire* launched a seemingly endless stream of sequels, spin-offs and imitators while revitalising the career of its star Lam Ching Ying. Lam would be forever linked to the grey-haired dynamic Van Helsing-style character, normally accompanied by bumbling assistants. *Mr Vampire* holds true to the edict "The original and still the best" with its effortless blend of genuine scares, slapstick and acrobatics. Mr Vampire himself is a towering gruesome hopping vampire whose every jump shudders the earth - a truly awe inspiring figure of fear. But the crucial card the film plays, is to offset his menace with 'Three Stooges' style kung-fu capers and mad special effects. After a manic opening, the film finds it stride by bombarding the audience with a bewildering array of myths, customs and weapons used in the control of the living dead. There is the chicken-blood soaked twine that can be used to bind a corpse to its coffin or create a shield, the flying sword of coins, incantations made with hastily precise calligraphy to curtail the corpse's movement and the inevitable sticky rice. Sticky rice is a perennial favourite of the genre with a variety of uses - it can be sprinkled liberally around to dissuade the casual hopping corpse (the effect is like burning coals to the bare footed dead), can draw out the poison in an infected wound or a single grain can be ignited for use in complex and dextrous spell casting. The only problem with sticky rice is that it is more expensive than the regular variety so inevitably some unscrupulous merchant will cut the goods to maximise profit - with catastrophic and often hilarious results. The film takes all of this in its stride as characters are thrown through walls, fly in the air and fight their way around feelingless corpses. All this and trouser removing gags, hideously mutilated necks, lychee twig cremations and a fog-bound, corpse-bearing carriage. Think Hammer, think Carry On, think kung-fu mayhem - *Mr Vampire* is your man.

93min, 15, Made In Hong Kong, Fang Factor Five.

Mr Vampire II (1986)

Dir: Sung Kan Shing

The first film's perfect blend of screams of laughter and screams of horror was going to be a tough act to follow - so they didn't bother! Part 2 is played far more for laughs than its predecessor though it still offers a jolt or two during the journey. One scene involves our heroes, trapped in a basement with a deadly hopping vampire only to have events exacerbated by the addition of slow-motion gas. Slow-motion gas does exactly what it says on the canister but, in a stroke of sheer genius, the director elected not to just film the chase in slow-mo, oh no, he gets everyone to act that way, greatly enhancing the humour of the scene due to its total lunacy and exaggerated expressions. Another chief source of amusement is the OK Kid, a traditional Chinese vampire child who is adopted by a group of children in a manner mirroring *ET*. In one musical interlude we follow the children at play, on swings and see-saws, with their new found friend wrapped up and wearing shades, and only perking up when they wheel him past a handy blood bank! While not in the same league as its forerunner there is still an awful lot to enjoy in *Mr Vampire II* and, like the first film, there's even a catchy song for you to sing along to as well. What more do you want? Blood?

85min, 15, Made In Hong Kong, Fang Factor Three.

The Musical Vampire (1990)

Dir: Wilson Tong Wai-Sing

St: Loletta Lee, Lam Ching-Ying

Two apprentice mortuary assistants Ah Hoo and Ah Keung, under the watchful eye of their incompetent nose-picking master, like nothing better than to play games with the recently deceased. Ah Hoo is charged with taking the corpse of Yam Ting-Tong to the village so that they can afford him proper burial rights but, as so often happens (well I find it does...), Yam is corpsenapped and sold to a Nobel Prize seeking French anatomist. One swapping of brain fluid later and Yam is liberated from normal vampiric restraints. As the body count rises Police Captain Tsao is given the task of capturing the errant vampire, so fits his sergeants with fang-proof collars and bright yellow curse sticks. What can possibly stop this relentless killing machine? As luck would have it Chu-Chu has a musical watch which pacifies her deceased relative by endlessly repeating *London Bridge Is Falling Down,* so they lay a trap... but Yam breaks the watch. The only thing left to do is to hire an ex-police orchestra of blind musicians to play or whistle the tune. Obvious really. That still leaves the problem of how to kill it - Taoist yellow umbrella merry-go-rounds and huge slabs of stone dropped from a great height have no effect, which leaves only acupuncture as a solution. But do you know all the pressure points, including the, ahem, naughty bits?

Utterly bonkers addition to the genre, like many it manages to be scary as well as very funny. It reaches its zenith in the scenes where Lam Ching-Ying sneakily tries every trick in the Taoist book to dispatch the hysterically whiny vampire. Everyone seems to be enjoying themselves immensely, hamming it uproariously and even managing to fit in a Benny Hill chase and a Monty Python-style 16 ton weight gag. Yam himself is both witty and gruesome as a vampire with an impressive set of tusk-like fangs. The final encounter is a real scream - even decapitation proves useless as Yam's disgruntled head frowns disapprovingly at his astonished assailant. When set up like an undead porcupine with acupuncture needles he looks genuinely pitiful but the coup de grâce is truly wince-inducing and very funny. Oh there are flaming pentagons, an outrageous rescue from firing squad, arms emerging from 30-foot poles, sudden scares, incompetent policemen and plenty of face slapping. Don't take it seriously (it sure as hell doesn't) and be prepared for a 90-minute shiver and giggle of a film. Madness at its best.

90min, Fang Factor Four.

Doctor Vampire (1991)

Dir: Q Xen Lee

In England Dr Chiang's car breaks down and he seeks shelter in a nearby castle, in fact a vampire brothel. He loses his virginity to Alice, who bites him in a very painful place. When her Master tastes the blood he declares it "like your Chinese ginseng" and demands that she goes to Hong Kong to fetch him. At the Chun Wa Medical Centre, Chiang brags about his sexual exploits to colleagues, being careful not to let Nurse May, his girlfriend, overhear. The centre needs the 3 doctors to step up their operation quota, which they do by giving Triad boss Mr Ta needless surgery ("You circumcised me because of a cold - now you want to remove my appendix because of a headache!") Chiang begins to turn, although he hasn't yet tasted human blood. May suspects that he is sleeping with sexy vamp Alice (he is, in his wardrobe!) so she concocts a love potion from her blood and feeds it to Chiang. Whoops!

A stunningly silly film in every way *Doctor Vampire* is laughter medicine, available without prescription. Hong Kong's Carry On Vamping misses nothing in its deconstruction of both the Western and Eastern vampire film, gleefully embracing all genres in its stride. Chiang's vampirism is Western, - "such things happen in Europe," and he wastes no time posing like Bela Lugosi but needs to maintain his identity, so is delighted to receive a traditional Chinese outfit from his colleagues and hop around for effect. Despite everyone's preoccupation with sex in the film it is there purely for seaside postcard humour. Where else can you see an undead boy scout staked with a broom, elephantine syringes of green acid squirted with manic enthusiasm, a glowing magical monk statue, a kung-fu gwailo master vampire, psychic blood transfusions and a battle between a medical laser and the laser-like stare of the Master? Mad, crass, hysterical - even when it's bad it's good. Take your medicine!

100min, Fang Factor Four and a tickled rib.

Vampire Settle On Police Camp (1990)

Dir: Chan Chi-Wah

St: Sandra Ng, Billy Lau, Alvina Kwong

Inspector Chan is having problems at work but it's his own fault. In a previous life he killed a family of 4 who are doomed to be vampires unless they can drag Chan to the King of Hell. They do this by terrorising the police training camp where Chan works with Officer Tong and the newly transferred brothel-buster Madame Lee. Chan seeks the aid of Wizard

Lousy who gives him the Nine Dragon Chasing Spellbook (available at all good newsagents) and says he needs 9 people of the same birth year to help defeat the curse. Which is where the new, naughty recruits come in. With July 14th approaching, a wild bunch of partying lecherous reprobates is all the help that Chan can find.

"It's a mess!" screams Madame Lee (playing the One Eyebrow Taoist Nun that is the film's Chinese title) towards the climax, and you find yourself agreeing with her assertion. Basically we are talking *Police Academy* with the addition of a family of vampires and a deluge of kung-fu. As the bungling boys ogle the aerobic-obsessed girls, the vampire father and grandpa join them for a while. Truly awful then but thankfully livened up by some acrobatic wirework and lots of people being smacked through doors. The vampires start the film off straight away with a horrific attack on the camp but seem impotent against the raw stupidity of the recruits. The only one with any chance is kid vamp, who breakdances, gets drunk, is great at fighting and surreally rides around the girls' dormitory on a stuffed giraffe ("Ah! Chinese ET" comments one) but suffers by picking up a glow-in-the-dark condom and having two men urinate glitter into his face. (Don't ask.) Madness on a budget, it seems as though the whole thing was made up on the spot with speeded up chases, sudden jump edits and excruciating sound. Not without its (police) campy charms though.

86min, 15, Videosino, Fang Factor One (ouch! that's my bum) oh all right, Two.

7. Vamping All Over The World

Asian Vampires

There's simply not enough space to delve deeply into the utter joys of world vampire films. We hope the following will produce a flavour of what's out there. Don't count on availability though, some of these are guaranteed to be hard to find and unlikely to be subtitled.

Malaya produced a series in the 50s, which became immensely popular. *Pontianak* (1956), *Dendam Pontianak* (1957), *Sumpah Pontianak* (1958), *Anak Pontianak* (1958), *Pontianak Kembali* (1963), *Pontianak Gua Musang* (1964).

Japan has been well known for its horror films including *Onna Kyuketsuuki* (1957), *Kyuketsuuki Ga* (1956) and *Kuroneko* (1968). Michio Yamamoto made a series of vampire films for legendary production company

ToHo (producers of Godzilla) - *Night Of The Vampire* (1970), *Lake Of Dracula* (1971) and *The Evil Of Dracula* (1975), which began to depict a more Western style of bloodsucker. The Japanese have also pioneered first class animation, anime, which may be classed as cartoons by some, but are far superior and definitely not for kids. They cover a wide variety of subjects, often science fiction and horror. The most easily obtainable vampire animes are *Dracula* (1980), *Vampire Hunter D* (1985) and *Vampire Princess Miyu* (1988).

South American Vampires

Mexico has a reputation of producing, er, somewhat strange films and their cinema audiences have long been vampire aficionados. In the 1950s, Fernando Mendez revived the genre with the imaginative *El Vampiro* (1957) and its sequel *El Ataud Del Vampiro (Vampires Coffin)* (1957), starring German Robles as a smoothy Count. The genre became immensely popular and countless further films were produced, some based on local legends, others being influenced by Hollywood films and yet more borrowed elements of science fiction and horror, producing some outlandish results. Most deranged of all though, were the wrestling films that have had an unsurpassed level of popularity. Wrestler Santo made several films where he fought a number of dastardly opponents, including Dracula and several other vampires, as well as werewolves, monsters, dwarves, mummies. If you can get 'em, try some of these: *Santo vs. The Vampire Women* (1961), *Santo And The Treasure Of Dracula* (1968), *Santo And The Vengeance Of The Vampire Women* (1969), *Santo And The Blue Demon vs. The Monsters* (1969), *Santo And The Blue Demon vs. Dracula And The Wolfman* (1972).

8. Pardon Me, But Your Teeth Are In My Neck

It's not all gloom and morbid longings for death. Successful comedy, like successful horror, relies on the premise that the characters you are watching are having a worse time than you are, or at least a different sort of bad time. With such a rich vein of lore to suck dry, comedy writers have plenty to get their teeth into. Batty sidelines include food (America's *Count Chocula* is still available, and in the UK there used to be cheese and onion maize *Fangs*), cartoons (Bugs Bunny in *Transylvania 6-5000*, *Count Duckula*, countless (sic) butlers in *Scooby Doo*) and even education (*Ses-*

ame Street's The Count), it seems as though nothing is immune from ridicule or commercialism.

Cinema horror spoofs have been around almost as long as the genre they parody. *Mother Riley Meets The Vampire* (John Gilling 1952), features the titular Riley (a 'popular' drag artiste of the Les Dawson school) who is falsely accused of murders committed by Lugosi's vampire and his horde of robots. Best not to question any further. The 60s saw most monster comedy on television as drive-ins were becoming more exploitational. There were shows like *The Munsters* with Al Lewis as Grandpa, a complaining OAP vampire (he reprised the role for New Zealand's *My Grandfather Is A Vampire* as a dead relative who can do wacky tricks) and *The Addams Family* with Carolyn Jones as the Vampira challenger Morticia, a role taken admirably by Angelica Huston in the excellent remakes. *Carry On Screaming* (1966) was pretty much what you'd expect. Veteran vampire John Carradine starred in the lamentable Philippino comedy *The Vampire Hookers* (Cirio Santiago, 1978) where the best gag was the teaser line "It's Not Blood They Suck." The 80s saw so many teen comedies a few vampire ones were inevitable. Some, like *Fright Night* or the incongruous Grace Jones stripping vampire flick *Vamp*, are more sassy horrors than outright comedies, but a beguiling number drift closer to laughter territory. *Transylvania 6-5000* (1985) (featuring pre-success roles for Jeff Goldblum and Geena Davies) has two hapless reporters searching for 'real' vampires in modern Transylvania, but sadly the scenery is the most interesting thing that the film has to offer. *Once Bitten* (1985) features 23-year-old Jim Carrey in an early role. In a crass excuse for sex gags, Lauren Hutton's Countess is on the hunt for virgin blood. In LA? You must be joking!

Abbott And Costello Meet Frankenstein (1948,USA)

Dir: Charles Barton

St: Budd Abbott, Lou Costello, Bela Lugosi

Dracula takes the role of Frankenstein in finding a suitable brain to reanimate a monster - the perfect brain apparently being in Lou Costello's head...

This film may be misnamed, but its amiable blend of jumps and goofing about go a long way to please an audience. Any worry that events are likely to drag is put aside by a stream of additional monsters into the pot - the wolfman (Lon Chaney) and even the invisible man (Vincent Price, uncredited) make appearances. The sets and make-up are great, due to Universal's tightly guarded copyright on its monsters. However the film's reputation diminished because of the rush of inferior sequels made in its wake. Watch the original. Even if you're not into the whacky duo, this is actually quite a good picture. It was one of Lugosi's last successes.

83min, Fang Factor Three.

The Fearless Vampire Killers (aka Dance Of The Vampires) (1967, UK)

Dir: Roman Polanski
St: Roman Polanski, Sharon Tate, Jack MacGowran

Professor Abronsius and his assistant Alfred have been travelling throughout Europe in search of vampires. They chance upon a remote village and meet some very strange locals. The bulbs of garlic hanging from the ceilings, the kidnapping of the innkeeper's daughter Sarah and the discovery of the innkeeper's frozen body complete with bite marks lead the Professor to continue his investigations at the local castle. They meet his Excellency and become convinced of his vampiric status, whereupon stakings and the rescue of Sarah become top priority. But His Excellency has organised a ball that evening and his son is very keen that young Alfred should attend...

Even before the start, where the MGM lion transforms into a vampire monster, you know this film is going to be a scream. Alfred and the archetypal wild-haired Professor travel though the moonlit snowscape, only to arrive at their destination with Abronsius frozen solid and are greeted by the weirdest villagers ever to grace a weird village. Alfred is a quiet observer, but also a coward and the Professor suitably bumbling until action is needed. When they arrive at the castle, His Excellency's knowledge of the Professor's work is as apparent as his son's (who looks like an extra from Fellini's *Satyricon*) appreciation of Alfred.

The great thing about this film is that it uses slapstick with subtlety and insight – most vampire spoofs establish the myths, then emphasise, re-emphasise and beat the joke into you some more. There's lots of visual comedy in *The Fearless Vampire Killers* – Alfred trying to break into the castle standing on the Prof's shoulders, who slowly sinks into the snow, and Abronsius getting stuck in the window of the crypt, legs sticking out and kicking frantically. The most famous joke concerns the Jewish vampire who, when confronted with a cross, shouts "Ayaah, you got the wrong vampire." Then there's the situation comedy – Abronsius and Alfred pretending to be vampires at the ball, dancing while they formulate and execute their plan to rescue Sarah. But they fail to notice a giant mirror that reveals only three people in the entire ballroom.

The film is also beautifully designed with glittering snowscapes, gothic castle and traditional peasant inn, complete with lashings of garlic. A total contrast to such films as *A Knife In The Water* and *Cul De Sac* from Polanski, but a very welcome one.

103min, 12, Warner Home Video, Fang Factor Five.

Love At First Bite (1979, USA)

Dir: Stan Dragoti
St: George Hamilton, Susan St James, Richard Benjamin

Dracula is comfy in his castle with Renfield until the Romanian authorities evict him and turn his pad into a gymnasium. Still it gives him the opportunity to emigrate to America and seek out the girl of his dreams - Cindy Sondheim, a model. Cindy is frankly a good-time girl but the Count's special brand of lurve is decidedly persuasive. This does not go down with Cindy's beau, psychiatrist Jeff, in fact a Van Helsing by birth.

Sporadically amusing lines and a couple of neat ideas are sprinkled through this distinctly average comedy but ultimately the 70s sensibilities and distasteful stereotyping drag it down. The romantic comedy aspect of the script works well but the actual execution is too insipid to realise its potential. Still Richard Benjamin's increasingly desperate attempts to destroy Hamilton (his failure when using silver bullets particularly futile) provide some relief as he spirals further down into insanity. Hamilton's Count is as smarmy as Frank Langella's from the same year but he remains the only character of interest by default - Renfield is irritating and Cindy is just trampy. A few nice touches (a blood-bank heist leads to the toast "here's blood in your eye" and a frustrating night of searching for victims leads to the Count becoming drunk on wino's blood and babbling maudlin nonsense to Renfield) can't raise the flagging whole.

93min, 15, Missing In Action, Fang Factor Two.

Dracula Dead And Loving It (1995, USA)

Dir: Mel Brooks
St: Mel Brooks, Leslie Nielsen

You know a genre has become a genre when Mel Brooks parodies it. However, this comedy look at the Dracula phenomena is an unsatisfactory affair. Taking his cue from cinematic sources as opposed to Stoker's novel the film none-the-less remains fairly close in structure to its literary predecessor. In terms of set design and lighting it's hard to fault, Brooks clearly knows his sources and milks them for all they are worth - the phantom carriage and doomed ship from *Nosferatu*, the ominous shadows of *Coppola's Dracula*, the castle from Tod Browning's, the mirror dance from *The Fearless Vampire Killers* and Mausoleum from any of Hammer's output. If it were simply a matter of spotting the reference then this would be great but sadly it's little more than a third rate *Young Frankenstein*. The good points are there: Nielsen is surprisingly deep in his portrayal of the Count, be it Lugosi drawl or the iconic stances of Christopher Lee; there are some great dance numbers; and the lighting/camerawork is wonderfully imitative. The fault lies in the fact that it is just not funny - tragic in a comedy. Despite the high production values give this a miss.

90min, PG, Fang Factor Two.

I Bought A Vampire Motorcycle (1989, UK)

Dir: Dirk Campbell
St: Neil Morrissey, Michael Elphick, Anthony Daniels

Nick Oddy (Noddy) thinks he's found a bargain when he buys a Norton Commando motorbike. Little does he know that its previous owner was killed by a rival gang whilst performing a bizarre demonic ceremony and the bike is now possessed. So when his best mate is murdered, the bike refuses to start in the daytime and his girlfriend is attacked, he suspects it's time to call a priest for help.

This is one silly little film that you can't help enjoying. Filmed in the West Midlands on a minuscule budget, it was produced at a time when the British film industry was really in the doldrums. The bike itself obeys all the vampiric conventions – keeps out of the daylight, has aversions to crosses and garlic, and sports a fine set of fangs and chomping headlights. There are oodles of jokes, although it does border on the puerile occasionally - the talking turd being a movement of note. But it's made with such genuine enthusiasm, everyone seems to be having a great time, Daniels and Elphick respectively hamming it up/deadpanning it to the max. Gory, silly and funny, it's a *Psychomania* for the 80s.

101min, 18, 4-Front, Fang Factor Three.

9. Offbeat Indies

What independent or alternative films lack in budget, they make up for with originality and a passion for the genre.

Count Yorga, Vampire (1970, USA)

Dir: Bob Kelljan
St: Robert Quarry, Roger Perry, Michael Murphy

Yorga, we are informed, "could not die by the mere passing of time" and can only be destroyed by a "miasma of putrid decay." He now conducts séances for Donna, and meets sceptical friend Paul and his girlfriend Erica. Following a car breakdown and a bit of rumpy pumpy in a camper, Erica is bitten by Yorga and starts developing the disconcerting habit of eating cats. Given the choice between a transfusion and Yorga's offer of "eternal love," Erica plumps for the latter and joins the Count's bevvy of buxom brides at his Spartan mansion.

Really the title gives it away. "Count Yorga" it announces, and then about a minute later, "Vampire." Swift is not the term for this. Nor subtle because we now know exactly what Count Yorga is, hence destroying any hint of intrigue the film may have had. *Count Yorga* was however, so successful that it spawned a sequel, countless (if you'll excuse the pun) imitators and launched the careers of Kelljan and Quarry. In some respects it is also a precursor for Frank Langella's stint as Dracula, as Yorga is oozy smoothy in the extreme. Unfortunately it is so deadly dull and flat you'll be hard pressed to see it through. It's the pacing and some atrocious 'pish bing' avant-garde muzak that really make it drag. The Count himself is so suave, polite and smarmy you want to throw up, but fortunately this is offset by a mad European sidekick called Brutar.

90min, Fang Factor Two.

The Return Of Count Yorga (1971, USA)

Dir: Bob Kelljan
St: Robert Quarry

"Have you seen Tommy?" Nope, but the undead have and put a temporary end to his annoying ball bouncing. At a sparse and tedious fancy dress party, Count Yorga gets his brides to gatecrash in a vain attempt to liven things up but it turns into a massacre and he is forced to hypnotise hostess Cynthia into forgetfulness. Suspicions are raised as the bodies are lowered in the nearby quicksand. Who should be on hand but marginally unstable Prof Riechsted with his crackpot ideas on vampirism?

Yorga's second charm offensive is exactly that - offensive - and his re-emergence is left thoughtlessly unexplained. Again Kelljan manages to come up with some inventive shots including a nice pink-toned flashback and a great ending, but also manages to make it drag and over-relies upon second-rate hand-held camerawork. There are some nice touches of humour - Yorga doesn't win the fancy dress party in his everyday clothes, but some upstart dressed as a second-rate vampire does.

92min, Fang Factor Two.

Guess What Happened To Count Dracula? (1970, USA)

Dir: Des Roberts
St: Des Roberts, Claudia Barron, John Landon

Count Adrian runs the themed bar Dracula's Dungeon, and is really a vampire with a remarkably bad goatee. Not that he's the only one with image problems - his establishment has every hippie drop-out, hunchback and wizened old hag in the neighbourhood queuing up to out-weird each other. Guy, a TV hotshot, and Angie go to a little soirée at Adrian's, but Adrian decides he wants Angie as a bride, wooing her with his cod-European accent. A visit to the laughing Dr Harris proves futile and Angie, now addicted to raw meat, is invited to the Macumbar Ritual - a stupifyingly dull dance of the mad, culminating in the chant of "eat the lizard."

Poverty row film in the wake of the inexplicably popular *Count Yorga*, this drive-in fodder is best left well alone. Red and green lighting is used so often you get the suspicion that perhaps it's meant to be 3-D. It isn't. Enlivened briefly by a (green) dream sequence and the line "Adrian, there's a gorilla in there" (there isn't, it's a guy in a gorilla suit) the raw gurning power is numbing. And you never find out what happened to Count Dracula, you have to guess. Cop out. Bargain basement, without the bargain.80min, Fang Factor One.

Blacula (1972, USA)

Dir: William Crain
St: William Marshall, Denise Nicholas

1780. Transylvania. Prince Mamawalda and his beautiful bride seek the abolition of the slave trade at Dracula's castle but the Count has other ideas. Changing the prince into a vampire he has him incarcerated to endure everlasting hunger, his bride to rot by his coffin, and even has the audacity to rename him Blacula. Fast forward to present day and two unscrupulous antique dealers have purchased Dracula's belongings for a song, including the prince. Big mistake. Blacula lives, kills the pair and starts feeding big time. He finds the spitting image of his bride in the shape of Tina, but being a gent he won't turn her unless she wants it. What a decent fellow.

At the height of Hollywood's blaxploitation phase came the atrociously named *Blacula* and concerns that the titular vamp would be a stereotypical jive-talking funkster. No need to worry, Blacula is probably cinema's most eloquent nosferatu with impeccable posture and diction. He also is a quick learner, spotting that photos taken of him would reveal his vampiric status, despite the fact he was incarcerated prior to photography's invention! So what we have is a socially conscious, intelligent aristocrat whose anachronistic attitudes single him out from the start. Marshall is great and the rest of the cast support him admirably, the script is tragicomic and only the average direction lets the side down. The climax has some nice stunt-work as our undead hero battles against the police, electrocuting one, chucking a couple down stairs and throwing barrels around with unbridled aggression. The ending is suitably poignant and noble. A hugely inferior sequel *Scream, Blacula, Scream* directed by Bob Kelljan killed off any chance of a long-running series with its tired clichés and plodding script.

90min, 15, Orion, Fang Factor Three.

Ganja And Hess (1973, USA)

Dir: Bill Gunn
St: Duane Jones, Marlene Clark

Dr Hess Green was stabbed three times - for the father, the son and the holy ghost - and now he has a habit to feed. Stealing blood from hospitals helps, but sometimes the craving for warm fresh corpuscles is too much to bear. What Hess needs is a companion to help him through this spiritually difficult time - which is where Ganja comes in.

A film with a tortured history *Ganja And Hess* was greeted warmly by Cannes critics and with incredulity from its distributors - they hacked over half an hour from the running time and tried to push the film as blaxploitation, relegating it to seedy drive-ins and video re-releases under a bewildering array of misleading titles. Now available as the director originally intended, it is clear why the distributors panicked - a 2-hour-long intelligent analysis of cultural and religious mores with cinematic nods to Van

Peebles, Passolini and 60s underground film-making was hardly likely to pack 'em in at the midnight triple bill. It does make for a thought-provoking piece that doesn't just bear repeat viewings, it demands them - right from the multiple voice over beginning shot in the New York Art Gallery. Gunn's assertion that blood is an intrinsic part of his cultural heritage is as intriguing as it is compelling. Matched with a rhythmic and evangelical score, this is a film to possess.

110min, All Day Entertainment (DVD R1), Fang Factor Four.

Martin (1977, USA)

Dir: George A Romero

St: John Amplas, Lincoln Maazel, Christine Forrest, Tom Savini

"Nosferatu - Vampire - First I will save your soul, then I will destroy you!"

Cuda is a fiercely religious old man, bound by a family curse to look after his cousin, an "84 year old going on 20" vampire. He wastes no time expressing his venom but Martin disputes his claims. Christina, Cuda's daughter, despairs at his bombastic fanaticism but there is reason for concern. Martin is a very troubled lad, cursed by visions of his past he sedates women, rapes them and drinks their blood. But is he a vampire or a delusional serial killer?

Romero revolutionised the horror movie with his debut *Night Of The Living Dead* (1969) so it was inevitable that eventually he would be convinced to make a vampire film. *Martin* is that film - quite unlike any other it remains his greatest achievement. The opening of the picture shows the full extent of Martin's crimes. It is meticulous, calculated and protracted. His sedative-filled syringes, held in his mouth like surrogate fangs, are a chilling image - even as he reassures his victims that everything is going to be alright you know it isn't. Murder is a messy business. Yet despite Martin's voyeurism, curt manner and unsavoury habits he still remains a figure of audience sympathy - his boyish looks and need-to-be-loved cries for help mean we want him to escape as much as we don't want him to kill. Cuda, with his white suits, cane and booming voice appears the real perpetrator - filling Martin's head with threats and wasting no opportunity to abuse him. What sets Romero's production apart is its grimness, believability and unwillingness to provide definitive solutions - by the end we are still unsure as to Martin's true vampiric roots. Flashbacks, in period black and white, provide Martin's dreampoint prior to periods of stress or elation, further compounding this uncertainty. The echoes of the past return to haunt him, even when he is the glibly named "The Count" on a trite phone-in show, the radio delay reverberates behind him like a bad memory. The film also seeks to address concerns about the decay of urban Pittsburgh, Romero's home town. A classic film in every sense, it can be read on multiple levels, each subsequent viewing revealing more.

94min, 18, Redemption, Fang Factor Five.

Subspecies (1990, Romania/USA)

Dir: Ted Nicolaou
St: Michael Watson, Laura Tate, Anders Howe

Two American research students visiting Transylvania become involved in a duel between two vampire brothers - one good, one evil - who are fighting to gain control of the powerful Bloodstone.

Funded with American money, but shot on location in Romania this is a surprisingly good little film. Clearly a labour of love from Nicolaou, it's a tale that truly celebrates the vampire lore of the region. The legend of the vampires adds an unusual twist and sympathetic tone to the film: after saving the village from Turkish invaders they still needed blood, so a gypsy ensured their supply by stealing the Bloodstone, infused with the life-force of the saints. The vampires and humans could then live in harmony. Naturally had the peace remained the film wouldn't be that exciting, so enter the evil dishevelled Radu, with Max Schreck fright-hands and dribbling double fangs, whose fingers drop off creating mini-fiends. He kills his own father, the king of the vampires, in order to win the Bloodstone.

Although the film was made cheaply, Nicolaou uses the natural beauty of the region with simple yet classy lighting effects and camera movements to create a more sumptuous feel. The Festival Of The Dead is shot with a passion, masks abound and horses ride over graves which are then staked in zealous ritual. The only criticism lies with the mini-fiend effects, which although well animated, Harryhausen style, are not composited precisely, but this is pedantic.

80min, 18, Entertainment In Video, Fang Factor Four.

Cronos (1992, Mexico)

Dir: Guillermo del Toros
St: Federico Luppi, Claudio Brook, Ron Perlman

A 16th century alchemist creates the Cronos device, a clockwork instrument that extends the user's life, at a price. Years later, tycoon De La Guardia and his nose-job obsessed delinquent offspring Angel seek the mechanism, which is now in the hands of Jesus Gris. Gris is an antique dealer who becomes addicted to the device which makes him youthful but also gives him a craving for human blood. Angel unwisely kills Gris, but back from beyond the grave and aided by granddaughter Aurora he seeks answers and revenge.

Del Toro's film is a magnificent curiosity, a gothic Mexican horror tale that engages from the opening. Ultimately it is a film about family love - Aurora tries to keep the Cronos device from Gris because she doesn't want to see her grandfather die an addict, but relents as she wants him to be happy. When he returns from the dead Aurora decks out a coffin-like chest with comfy rugs so he can sleep. All would be cosy were it not for 2 things - Gris is a walking decomposing corpse with a need for blood, and there's a sick man's son on his trail. Perlman is in his element as Angel, first seen by the family asking advice on which shape of nose suits him best whilst trying to purchase the statue that contained the device. More notable is del Toros' use of insects, a trait that would serve him well later in his career directing the large budget Hollywood bug flick *Mimic*. Despite the close-knit casting (this is essentially a 5 person film) there is room for a fine support character - the mad mortician, an artist with a particularly wicked sense of humour. When Angel asks to see Gris' body, he points to the crematorium oven and says "well done or medium rare?" Superbly lit and underplayed by all bar Perlman (this is a compliment!) this is a strangely moving film, at times morbid and sticky but never exploitational. Marvellous and original.

88min, 18, Tartan Video, Fang Factor Five.

Bloodstone: Subspecies II (1993, Romania/USA)

Dir: Ted Nicolaou
St: Anders Hove

Radu returns, stitched together by his mini-pals, and stakes his brother. Michelle, bitten in Part One, tries to get out by train but public transport is no cure for the call of the undead as Radu demands the return of the Bloodstone. Rebecca, her sister, is determined to discover Michelle's fate so, teaming up with a professor and American ambassador Mel, they head off to Radu's pad. But Radu's mum, a hideous sorceress is waiting...

The action moves from the country to the city (Bucharest) and back but Nicolaou has lost none of his ability to light a scene in the transition. Whether it's the backlit forests of the film's opening or huge menacing shadows cast dynamically over buildings the effect is startling, realism has nothing to do with it. Once again this is a fine advert for Romania, the architecture and countryside are beautiful yet mysterious and the plum brandy (Plinka) looks very tasty. Moving on from the mythic dread of Part One we begin to see the basis of a vampire soap opera emerging. Make sure you have Part Three on hand before watching this as it does end on a semi-cliffhanger. Really there is nothing to fault the film apart from what remains a highly uninspiring title.

84min, 18, CIC, Fang Factor Three.

Bloodlust: Subspecies III (1993 Romania/USA)

Dir: Ted Nicolaou
St: Anders Hove

Fledgling Michelle hates Radu's eternal love, but she's eager to learn how to use her newly-blossomed powers, if only to give her a better chance of escape. Becky is still having problems with police inspector Marin not believing her story but has made some progress with Mel, enough for him to ship over CIA cameo man Bob with his Milk Tray man abseiling antics. With a little luck and a lot of weaponry they might be able to wrest Michelle from Radu's substantial fingers.

Centuries have not improved Radu's eating habits, he really is a mucky pup when it comes to food. All dribble, and he will insist on talking with his mouth full. Also his wooing techniques leave a great deal to be desired - still his love is strong enough to kill his own mum. Oh the angst. Nicolaou's command of in-camera trickery reaches new heights in his portrayal of fast vampire movements, they are breathlessly smooth and reminiscent of the pre-sound pioneers. Another impressive score of folk and orchestral helps gloss over the budget limitations as does a remarkable and graphic denouement from the castle walls - just imagine what this guy could do with a Hollywood paycheque!

79min, 18, CIC, Fang Factor Three.

Embrace Of The Vampire (1994, USA)

Dir: Anne Goursaud
St: Martin Kemp, Alyssa Milano, Jennifer Tilly

Centuries after being feasted upon by three water nymphs, The Vampire is searching for "my love, my virgin" before he falls into an eternal sleep. She, it turns out, is nun-raised Charlotte, whose friends know that what she needs is sex, as does her boyfriend Chris. The Vampire appears every night - soft, caressing, passionate, slowly encroaching into her life. Even the gift of a crucifix cannot avail, electing for the Vampire's ankh it seems that Charlotte's life and Chris' aspirations are drifting away.

Despite being well shot and pleasantly sound mixed, the initial draw of *Embrace Of The Vampire* remains seeing Eastenders and ex-Spandau Ballet man Kemp making an arse of himself in a ropey vampire flick. He's not bad, but his smooth "Come to me Charlotte" murmurings are fairly nausea inducing. Credibility is not the film's strong point. However it is an amiable little number with some fine art direction from the Timotei school of advertising and a solid supporting cast. The plot is familiar to anyone who has read a Mills and Boon novel - take one virginal girl with a nice boyfriend, let her dally with a love-machine, wrestle with her conscience and finally return to the good man having *just* avoided sex with the desirable aristocrat for whom she secretly yearns for the rest of her life. Wholesome to the core despite the substantial nudity, you'll either love the diffused forest shots with dreamy floaty feathers (think *Legend* and you're nearly there) or throw up. Secretly, we liked it.

88min, 18, Medusa, Fang Factor Three.

Nadja (1994, USA)

Dir: Michael Almereyda
St: Elena Lowensohn, Suzy Amis, Peter Fonda

Nadja has fallen out with her brother Edgar, who wants to find an alternative to their vampire ways. She seduces Lucy but trouble is at hand because Lucy's husband Jim is in with Ben, a slightly psychotic vampire hunter with a penchant for mirrored spectacles and bicycle clips. A standoff is inevitable. But will it be in America or Romania, ancestral home of the Ceaucescu Draculs?

A low-budget independent feature film executive produced by David Lynch (who appears briefly as a police officer), *Nadja* was never going to be to everyone's taste. Director Michael Almereyda made his name by shooting art films on a Fisher Price toy video camera that produces low resolution black and white pixilated images - a technique that is prevalent during much of the overt vampiric activity in the film. This complements the traditional film stock perfectly and creates a genuine sense of 'otherness' - the technique accentuates the counter-normality of the occurrences, it's almost hallucinatory at times. The relationships between all the main characters is tight, each attached to the others through at most one intermediary. There is far more to *Nadja* than underground aesthetics and philosophical discourse. It revels in both film and vampire lore. Nadja's slave is called Renfield, her victim Lucy, her family are from the Dracul line - but the names are more than just homage to Dracula, it is no coincidence that Edgar's amour is called Cassandra. Nadja herself harks back to Garbo, in speech and expression ("Sometimes I want to be alone"), and certainly in perceived sexual ambivalence and androgynous beauty. The main strength of the vampire shown here is that of persuasion, the melting of wills over lesser mortals. Nowhere is this talent more apparent than within the changing Lucy, whose growing powers are so strong she can successfully hail a cab. In New York! The real character of the film is Ben the vampire hunter, who appears far worse than those he hunts. This bicycle-riding, stake-wielding psychopath thinks nothing of killing poor old Bela the spider and has an unusual method for spotting vampires in his mirrored shades. If there is a problem with *Nadja* it lies with a need to provide political comment on contemporary events in Romania and somehow link this to the theme of vampirism, which is inappropriate. That said, *Nadja* is that rare breed, an art film that entertains as well as stimulates.

88min, 15, ICA, Fang Factor Four.

Night Owl (1994, USA)

Dir: Jeffrey Arsenault
St: John Leguizamo

Jake "doesn't need to rebel against anything." What he does need is to pick up girls in trendy clubs, have sex with them, drink their blood and dump them into black plastic bags. He also takes to drinking his own blood in an attempt to curb his hunger, to little avail. But a victim's brother is on his tail.

Bathrooms have long held a fascination with horror film-makers. The blend of vulnerability, bodily functions, privacy and nudity prove an irresistible mix, the ideal location for scary happenings. The zenith of bathroom horrors remains *Psycho*, the violation of Norman stabbing Marion as much sexual as murderous. *Night Owl* takes this premise to its blatant extreme in that Jake has sex with his victims on the sink prior to offing them. It's as dingy as the cinematography. Murky 16mm shot entirely with available light - a laudable concept but one that hasn't really worked. For a film made in 1994 it has all the feel of a drive-in beatnik flick complete with grotty basement clubs and a ludicrous 'shock' poetess/rapper called Screamin' Rachel. Sadly the squalid crimes and hairy butts do little to pique the interest, leaving a nasty taste.

73min, 18, Screen Edge, Fang Factor Two and a bit (for Caroline Munroe who makes a pointless but fascinating cameo).

The Addiction (1995, USA)

Dir: Abel Ferrera
St: Lili Taylor, Christopher Walken

Kathleen is a philosophy student with a doctoral thesis to deliver and a thirst for human blood. The latter was the result of an alleyway attack by an aggressive female vampire. Now she has taken to dark shades and corpuscular slurpings, not that this is entirely bad for her as it provides practical application for her ethics paper.

Take your happy hat off now. Abel Ferrera, no-nonsense guerrilla filmmaker that he is, has crafted a relentlessly bleak and harrowing tale of urban vampirism which takes on genocide, drug addiction, massacres and the propensity for humankind to perpetuate atrocity without remorse. Not a date flick then. To enhance the desolation Ferrera decided to shoot entirely in unflinching black and white, emphasising shadows, blood and despair. Juxtaposing Kathleen's decline into vampirism with images of the Holocaust and America's atrocities towards the Vietnamese, hammers home the film's fundamental message - evil is made by guiltless people and allowed to happen by the weak will of others - by doing nothing you are complicit in the suffering. Kathleen is made a vampire because of her lack of strength at facing up to her oppressor. Paradoxically she is not alive, any more than the drug addicts that provide the film's other metaphor, a point emphasised by a wildly overacting Christopher Walken. Ferrera's film is lean enough to hold onto the viewer but the ceaseless barrage of soundbite philosophy and harrowing imagery is as draining on the viewer as Kathleen's bite. Sobering.

82min, 18, Pathé, Fang Factor Three.

Vampire Journals (1996, USA)

Dir: Ted Nicolaou
St: Jonathon Morris, David Gunn, Kirster Cerre

Zachary is "God's most desolate creature - a vampire with a compassionate heart" driven to vengeance by the death of his beloved Rebecca. He has the blade of Laertes with which he intends to dispatch arch vampire Ash. But he didn't expect to fall in love again, with Liszt-playing pianist Sophia. Ash gets Sophia to play for him and offers her the prospect of eternal life. She declines, but this doesn't stop him having a nibble anyway. A face-off is inevitable but, with Ash holding Sophia's soul, are the scales weighed too heavily against the angst-riddled decapitator?

The stupendously low budget, the over-reliance on voice-overs and the presence of TV-sitcom actor Morris (*Bread* - Heaven forbid!) makes for grim portents. Add the marginally silly premise of an anti-vampire vampire to the equation and the gut reaction is to avoid this one like the plague. If you did however, you would be missing one of the most unexpectedly decent vampire films of recent years. Director Nicolaou (*Subspecies*) turns the budget limitations to his advantage by extensive and impressive use of shadows and jump-cuts to portray the movement, metamorphosis and power of the vampires. Indeed virtually the whole film is a lighting dream with exquisite use of colour to define mood and dynamic, occasionally moving, light sources. Zachary is another of cinema's reluctant vampires "I drink in shame...I dare not face my prey" - but redeems himself by being an A-class decapitator. Normal vampires can be destroyed in the standard manner but a master vamp like Ash can only crumble into dust if caught in the ecstasy of feeding - which fortunately for Zachary happens with alarming regularity. Aside from the artistic merits of the production, we are not short changed when it comes to vampiric habits - heads roll, necks get bitten and there's oodles of writhing bodies and spurting blood, just what the doctor ordered. Steeped in mythic convention yet with enough twists to keep you on your toes *Vampire Journals* is an unexpected surprise, akin to finding a diamond in a Kinder egg.

78min, 18, Entertainment In Video, Fang Factor Four.

Razorblade Smile (1998, UK)

Dir: Jake West
St: Eileen Daly, David Warbeck

Lilith Silver is a hit woman by day and fraternises with imitation vampires in seedy clubs by night, mainly to relieve the boredom of being able to live for eternity. She becomes involved with killing members of an Illuminatus sect, who are naturally rather irritated and thus begins a game of cat and mouse which may lead her into more danger than she realises.

A British production filmed on a small budget, but with access to decent post production equipment, *Razorblade Smile* is a film made with genuine love and affection for the genre. Lilith looks delicious in her full fetish gear, and tells her story direct to the camera, dispelling or confirming the various myths when she sees fit. She grades her victims' blood, depending on how tasty a quaff they produce - the hit is pretty poor quality, even the lesbian vampire wannabe only gets a B+. So who's got the A grade blood? The plot is tight, the pacing right for the chase scenes and there's a genuine twist at the end. It's well designed, loud and looks great, even the credits are stunning. However, there's something lacking and unfortunately it probably lies with the performances. The enthusiasm of all involved is plain to see, but with the exception of David Warbeck, no one seems particularly animated. Well, they are dead I suppose.

18, Manga Entertainment, Fang Factor Three (B+ for effort).

The Wisdom Of Crocodiles (1999, UK)

Dir: Po Chih Leong

St: Jude Law, Elena Lowensohn, Timothy Spall

Stephen Grlscz needs only two things in life - love and a surname with vowels. Unfortunately the love he needs flows from the blood of his partners, nurtured sensitively - he is the perfect boyfriend were it not for his killing embrace. Such behaviour cannot go unnoticed forever and Inspector Healey is on the case. As Grlscz begins the ritual anew with Anne he faces an unexpected problem - what happens if he begins to love his victim as much as she loves him?

Have you ever wondered what 'good causes' have benefited from your lottery ticket purchases? Well here's one, a cracking piece of thoughtful cinema where nothing is wasted and everything links. Jude Law is ideal material for the mysterious and moody vampire exuding tenderness until his violent streak pervades. He keeps detailed diaries of all the women he encounters, gathering pieces of their lives, possessions and emotions to keep in an eternal scrapbook. When he feeds, it is not just his victim's blood that he drinks, it is also their love and feelings - his body rejects the negative emotions as crystalline deposits - can a love be pure and uncontaminated? Which is where Anne comes in - beautiful and intelligent she has philosophical and practical qualities and a similar detached view of the world. She is the one that Grlscz will find hard to kill, because she draws emotion from him. And what of the crocodiles? Grlscz has the reptilian third of his brain dominant, and as such is a predator - at times he crouches like a crocodile, contemplating his next move, waiting for his next kill. His love is as calculated as his body disposals - crocodile love with crocodile tears and an infectious smile. Intelligent, complex and marvellous.

95min, 18, Entertainment In Video, Fang Factor Four.

10. Deranged And Confused

There are some very strange films out in the big wide world and vampire films have their fair share. Did you know that William Shatner made a vampire film called *Incubus* (1965) and that all the dialogue was in Esperanto? How about *The Deathmaster* (1972), where a vampire becomes guru to a bunch of hippies? Or Andy Warhol's *Blood For Dracula*, featuring Udo Kier searching for the blood of virgins in Catholic Italy. There's the psychedelic *Chappaqua* (1966) by Conrad Rooks, with William Burroughs, Allen Ginsberg and Ravi Shanker. Some are good, some bad, some indifferent, all are bizarre...

Zoltan: Hound Of Dracula (aka Dracula's Dog) (1977, USA)

Dir: Albert Band
St: Michael Pataki, Jan Shuton, Jose Ferrer
A Russian soldier removes a stake protruding from a veiled body - it stirs, leaps and kills. It is Zoltan, hound of Dracula! The motley mutt plays fetch with the stake protruding from servant Schmidt and the pair seek the last surviving Dracula. He is Michael Drake, forced into exile two years ago - strange as he's already raised a family and performed a remarkable feat of disguising his Russian accent. The family are on a camping holiday unaware their lakeside vacation will turn into a terrifyingly tedious set of canine encounters.

Bad dog! Bad, bad dog of a film. Zoltan marks the nadir in poor canine vampire action, his glowing white eyes no match for his gleeful trot. Often a glove puppet, often a fake paw on a stick, always an inscrutable bore, this doggy doomster drags on forever. Interminable scenes of family life are sub-Disney and whenever the terror begins it's mainly minutes of dogs howling. The night scenes are cut between daytime shots so you're never really sure what's happening anyway. Compounded by a dated muzak score, a failure on everyone's part to at least fake an accent, the plodding script, lame direction and tired gore effects (by Stan Winston the credits say, unbelievable) and a ludicrous *Night Of The Living Dogs* siege in a fisherman's hut, means you are advised to put this one down. Permanently.
83min, 18, Warner Home Video, Fang Factor One.

The Lair Of The White Worm (1988, UK)

Dir: Ken Russell

St: Amanda Donohoe, Hugh Grant, Peter Capaldi

The D'Ampton worm, steeped in myth, is ready to feed on virginal blood once more. Sylvia Marsh serves as high priestess to the vampiric snake cult, her reptilian charms and infectious poison turning the countryside population into fanged servants of the worm Dionin. Angus the archeologist, Mary and Eve whose parents mysteriously disappeared a year ago, and new lord of the manor James D'Ampton, combine to stop the menace. With the aid of old 78 records and Angus' bagpipes, they set about luring the slinky snake.

Based very loosely on Bram Stoker's novel, Ken Russell's film is a deliriously camp homage to the low-budget British horror film but imbued with his own inimitable style. Mixing all the clichés with gay abandon, the deliberately stilted dialogue and boyish desire to offend is as infectious as Donohoe's delicious venom. She is simply marvellous as Sylvia, vamping her performance as she slinks around in a variety of costumes. Whether spitting venom at crucifixes, sinuously dancing uncontrollably to music or burning her snakes and ladders board to the lament "Rosebud," she dominates any shot she's in. Grant's performance is so reprehensible, it merely adds a further dimension to a character who is ineffectual at best. But the real star of the show is Russell himself as writer, director and producer showing that age has not mellowed his impish enfant terrible reputation. Anything vaguely snakelike, be it vacuum attachment or hose, is brought to life and Sylvia's infectious venom causes outrageous hallucinations. These dayglow video tableaux are mini-masterpieces of appalling taste recalling Russell's earlier *Altered States*. James' dream of entering the worm's cavern is no less bizarre - visions of Sylvia and Eve wrestling as air stewardesses while he is strapped to the chair. "You're bonkers" says Angus and who can argue? Gleefully, outrageously naughty and misunderstood by virtually everyone, this is another classic slice of utter madness from Britain's most underappreciated auteur.

96min, 18, First Independent Video, Fang Factor Four and a squirt.

Addicted To Murder (1995, USA)

Dir: Kevin J Lindenmuth

St: Mick McCleery, Laura McLauchlin, Sasha Graham

Joel Winters, aka The New York Mangler, is half Henry from *Eraserhead*, half *Henry Portrait of a Serial Killer* as his confused sexuality causes him to kill. Subject of intense media interest, his life is dissected and examined. And then there was Rachel. Rachel loved to be killed again and again - phallically chainsawed, stabbed, electrocuted - all the more ecstatic because, being a vampire she could repeat the whole process the next day. But Rachel left him and he needed a substitute, willing or not.

Audaciously mixing television's propensity for sound-bite psychoanalysis and false disgust at the process of murder with the fragmented life and loves of serial killer Joel, *Addicted To Murder* can't be accused of triviality. Ignoring linear coherence to distort the world in Joel's eyes, the combination of Nicholas Roeg influenced editing and social critique make for a thought-provoking, if queasy, experience. The acting is uniformly excellent and the television shows that sporadically sprinkle the film are convincing. Any problem lies squarely with the format - BetaSP - which renders the image flat and insipid, a necessity of the obviously low budget. It's a brave attempt at filming a different kind of vampire tale with verve and tenacity.

90min, 18, Screen Edge, Fang Factor Three.

Darkness (1995, USA)

Dir: Leif Jonker
St: Gary Miller, Michael Gisick, Cena Donham

Toby is mulling around a petrol station convenience store when a bloodied man announces "He's coming" and blows his own head off with a captured police handgun. 'He' is the Evil One, head of the vampires with a dusty trench coat and waist-length hair to match. One massacre and 3 days later Toby is a 100% certified vampire hunter. Teaming up with a group of kids, they have only one thing to do: Survive.

After the success of *El Mariachi* it became fashionable to advertise how little your film had cost. Leif Jonker's *Darkness* is a classic contender, weighing in at a lean $6,000 but looks and feels a great deal more. As is fitting for a production funded partly by the writer/director selling his blood, this is an exceptionally violent splatterfest, borrowing liberally from Romero's *Dawn Of The Dead* and Kauffman's remake of *Invasion Of The Body Snatchers*. Bodies are shot to pieces, chainsawed, burnt, splatted by vehicles and all manner of unpleasantries rendered with highly effective make-up and in-camera effects – it puts many large budget productions to shame. The characters do the sensible thing by sticking together which makes any death seem all the more tragic. Jonker constantly keeps on his toes by judicious, unusual editing, Carpenter-style sideways tracking and a barrage of inventive camera angles. The huge cast of friends and locals do a fine job of keeping the tension rolling as they generally head towards damnation and a sticky ending. Never dull, always inventive, gains an extra fang for nerve and persistence.

90min, 18, Screen Edge, Fang Factor Four.

Sucker The Vampire (1998, USA)

Dir: Hans Rodionoff
St: Yan Birch, Monica Barber

Plasma are a rock group that are getting too successful - they are only in it for the groupies' blood. Lead singer Anthony breaks up the band but need not have bothered because the vengeful Miss Vanessa Helsing is dispatching the rest of the group. Anthony has an able helper in the shape of Reed who disposes of the nubile young corpses via his handy hospital job. After he's taken photographs of himself with the stiffs in increasingly outlandish lingerie, of course. All tables are turned however when Anthony contracts AIDS.

It's a Troma film. Normally this is as much as needs to be said, but this one proves to be an inventive stab at low-budget modern vampirism. Gone are the extreme gore effects that generally lighten up Troma's output and instead you are left with a knowing tongue-in-cheek script that is tight and normally funny. Occasionally the tasteless elements look like veering into taboo areas, but the film-makers just manage to avoid it by adopting a gleefully macabre tone to the proceedings. The spectre of *Buffy The Vampire Slayer* appears in the shape of the punnily-named Vanessa Helsing but the film subverts expectations with her early demise. Hugely enjoyable is Reed, the mad hunchbacked assistant without the hunchback, whose $30 purchases of tacky goods (a rubber stake and hammer) and disturbing sexual practices make him a far more interesting character than the ostensibly dull Anthony. With a hip jokey indie soundtrack (*Graveyard Girlfriend* plays over Reed's photography and *Love Is Dead* gets an airing) and some nice exchanges ("I'm a vampire" - "I know, you're a lawyer") *Sucker* is not art but it's a great laugh. Filmed in Ponceovision. After cinematographer Poncin, naturally...

89min, 18, Fang Factor Four.

11. Sci-Fi Suckers

The vampire genre declined in the 40s and 50s as Sci-Fi B-movies were becoming the rage. It was easy to see why. The Cold War was kicking in and monster movies reflected fears about the atomic age. Vampires however could also be considered to be monsters, and the genre was subverted. Consequently numerous films were released which involved bloodsucking fiends in other forms - and often from outer space. *The Thing From Another World* (1951) featured an alien frozen in ice which, when revived, needed human blood to propagate its species. *Bloodsuckers* (1966) featured a vampiric tree and *Little Shop Of Horrors* (1960, remade in 1986) similarly included a bloodsucking plant. Mario Bava's astonishing and disturbing *Planet Of The Vampires* (1965) told the story of a space captain who crash-landed on a planet where the inhabitants were dead, but rose to destroy the living, providing a partial template for Ridley Scott's *Alien*.

The Omega Man (1971, USA)

Dir: Boris Segal
St: Charlton Heston, Anthony Zerbe

In 1975 a virulent plague turned the population into night dwellers with pallid skin and spooky eyes. All apart from Neville, a scientist who had developed a powerful anti-virus that he selfishly used only on himself. Two years later he spends the day talking to himself and exterminating vampires. At night he defends his fortress home from the vampire hordes. But having discovered the last gasp of humanity, each slowly developing the symptoms, Neville can either develop a serum from his immune blood or use the fact that he's the only "real man" to his advantage and start spreading his seed.

Based in part on Richard Matheson's book *I Am Legend* (which had already been made into *The Last Man On Earth* (1964) starring Vincent Price) *The Omega Man* is a big budget action film with unforgivable pretensions. What could have been simple but enjoyable entertainment is ruined by ham-fisted religious symbology and anti-Communist messages. This is from a film that substantially altered its source because stakes are boring, but good traditional US gunfire is what represents the freedom of the individual. Heston really is too old for this. His remarkable chat-up lines ("If you were the only girl in the world and I, hey I am the only boy, baby") are only succeeded by his uncanny ability to adopt sombre crucifix stances. It makes his nemesis Matthis all the more appealing. You start believing his assertion that Neville is nothing more than a mass murderer.

At least the action is adequate and you do see Heston suffer extensively twice, so it's not all bad.

94min, PG, Warner Home Video, Fang Factor Two.

Lifeforce (1985, USA)

Dir: Tobe Hooper
St: Frank Finlay, Mathilda May

Following the trail of Halley's Comet the Churchill comes across a 150-mile-long spaceship. Inside they discover and recover weird fossilised bat creatures and three humanoid bodies. When the Churchill returns to Earth the crew have died, shrivelled like walnuts. Before long 3 hard-kissing naked vampires from outer space are spreading their own kind of love around the fair capital, turning its denizens into exploding bloodlust mad-things. Meanwhile the silently drifting incubator moves inexorably towards Earth and dominance of the human race.

Lifeforce is the stuff of legends. Take one successful director (fresh from *Poltergeist* and *Salem's Lot* but with enough cred from *Texas Chainsaw Massacre* to pull it off), a cracking genre scriptwriter (O'Bannon, of *Alien*, *Dark Star*, and *Return Of The Living Dead* fame) and a special effects genius (John *Star Wars* Dykstra) and throw them an unprecedented sum of hard cash. It cost a fortune, it lost one too. Its main flaw remains that it is a very silly, but hugely enjoyable B-Movie smothered with big budget effects. And what effects they are, a stunning combination of optical and prosthetic work - when some poor unfortunate gets drained you see it all before your very eyes, no dissolves or cuts. The earlier sequences in the alien spacecraft are superb, Hooper making the best of his wide canvas to portray the drifting astronauts dwarfed by the organic hive-like surroundings. Chiefly, however, it's still remembered for its prime concept - naked chick kills people, a grade-Z exploitation device. Cheesy to the point of full maturity it takes a lot to dislike a film that includes the line "She killed all my friends and still part of me didn't want to leave." Awfully good.

97min (116), 18, VCC, Fang Factor Three.

Vampirella (1996, USA)

Dir: Jim Wynorski
St: Talisa Soto, Roger Daltry, Richard Joseph Paul

Thirty centuries ago, on Drakulon, renegade vamps led by Vlad escape imprisonment for drinking living blood, killing the Council. Ella swears revenge and follows them to Earth. The vamps have an enemy in the shape of Operation Purge, whose main operative is Adam Van Helsing. Our scantily clad heroine is just ready to dispatch Vlad when they are both captured by Purge. Convincing Adam she is a non-life threatening vampire due to a special armband they unite. But Vlad has plans for Judgement Day when a satellite-induced nuclear winter will allow the vampire hordes (who seem to number about 30) to rule.

Based on the comic series, the presence of Roger Corman in the credits goes a long way to explain the B-movie charms of this tight little production. Vampirella has a marginally more practical outfit than her pen-and-inked counterpart but fortunately maintains the ludicrous white collars and "raven-haired charms." However the real star of the show is Roger Daltry, relishing his role as evil vamp Vlad. Replete with ghastly fangs that change size frequently, this is not Daltry's first encounter with vampirism - he appeared opposite Paul Nicholas' full-fanged Wagner in Ken Russell's masterfully deranged biopic *Lisztomania*. Roger tackles his role with pantomime theatricals and hysterically overdone cloak swishing. This is all part of the knowing humour and B-Grade aesthetics - Vampirella asks to be chained up to prevent her from biting Adam, vampy vamp Sallah wastes no opportunity to wiggle her wares, Vlad's ability to mind-control a driver leads to pointlessly funny car stunts and the whole shebang is drenched with cod-scientific explanations. Like a cheap version of Mike Hodge's camp classic *Flash Gordon* mixed with an episode of *Wonder Woman*, *Vampirella* is pure hokum that is amusing when intentional and hysterical when not.

82min, 15, Warner Home Video, Fang Factor Two, Camp Factor Five.

12. Bloody Hollywood

Vampire films in Hollywood are a bit like buses, you can wait a few years, then several come along at once. The ebb and flow of production follows audience trends as is to be expected in a commercial environment. Many respected Hollywood directors have had a stab at the genre - Coppola, Scott, Carpenter, Bigelow, Landis amongst others. The main difference between these and most of the other films covered so far is that the majority of Hollywood movies have a substantially larger budget.

The Night Stalker (1971)

Dir: John Llewellyn Moxey
St: Darren McGavin

Shirley Hughes is "on route to her doom," the first of a succession of women who are attacked and drained of blood. A news story for reporter Kolchak, if his editor Vincenzo will print it and the police accept that a vampire is responsible. When a hospital blood bank is raided and police bullets have little effect on the perpetrator, they begin to take notice of Kolchak's madcap theories.

When first broadcast *The Night Stalker* became the most watched TV Movie in the US up to that point. In retrospect it is easy to see why, but is nonetheless so deeply flawed that it provides virtually no entertainment. First off is Kolchak himself. You can't shut up his ceaseless patter - on and on like a bad cabby he peppers you with meticulously pointless detail and hard-nosed reporter similes. The murders are all very 70s - girls in hot pants and bad shirts who work in clubs deserve to die, whilst sensible woman in lemon flares with Doberman deserves to live but only after being tortured. Some of the action sequences do liven things up a bit, but when a hospital orderly is chucked out of a window the otherwise impressive stunt is ruined by sight of the crashmat - shoddy. *The Night Stalker* does gain an extra fang purely on the basis o^f having the most tasteless credit sequence of all time - an autopsy shot from the corpse's point of view which pulls off the rare feat of being gratuitous, protracted and yet shows nothing. The film's success led to a further movie, *The Night Strangler* and a short lived TV Series, *Kolchak: The Night Stalker* with a 'monster of the week' style format.

Fang Factor Two.

Salem's Lot (1979)

Dir: Tobe Hooper
St: James Mason, David Soul

Writer Ben Mears returns to his home town of Salem's Lot. He is not the only recent resident. Straker, partner of the elusive Mr Barlow, has purchased the super-creepy Marsden house and establishes an antique shop. Before long the Glick boys disappear only to re-emerge as floating vampires under the power of the exceptionally bald and blue Mr Barlow. It takes little time for an epidemic to spread and only 3 people are brave, or stupid enough to try to defeat the menace - horror film fan Mark, Ben, and his new found girlfriend Susan.

Originally a hugely popular mini-series, Hooper's version of Stephen King's first novel was re-edited to fit the time constraints of a feature film. Sadly this diminishes the creeping eeriness of the series that relied far more on mood than shock tactics. Hooper's attention to set design mirrors that of his groundbreaking debut *The Texas Chainsaw Massacre* with the Marsden house fitted out with stuffed animals and a feel of putrefaction. Even if the scares are a bit "da-da" and designed to fit advertising breaks, their effect is still jolting. Mr Barlow is a hideous feral creature of dominating stature and a Schreck-like screen presence, a formidable and memorable figure. However even he is dwarfed by Mason's superbly droll performance as Straker, who gets all the best lines too - "You'll enjoy Mr Barlow - and he'll enjoy you." His all too human death is played out with aplomb and a great deal of shock. If that were not enough, Hooper's child vampires are amongst the creepiest ever, floating in the mist and scratching endlessly at windows, the sound alone is disturbing. Soul is bearable as the hero but his sidekick Mark is great as the teen on the edge who survives because of his love of Lon Chaney flicks. Hooper makes more than a nod to Hitchcock too, the Marsden house is filmed in a similar manner, and the use of stairs is shot identically to scenes in *Psycho* and *Notorious*. The addition of Harry Sukman's Hermannesque score merely adds to the feeling. If possible seek out the TV print which allows the real sense of an isolated community to shine through.

105min, 18, Warner Home Video, Fang Factor Four.

The Hunger (1983)

Dir: Ridley Scott

St: Catherine Deneuve, Susan Sarandon, David Bowie

As old as the Pharaohs, Miriam feeds her immortality on the blood of the living, slashing them with an ankh knife and destroying the bodies in her basement crematorium. Her companions remain with her for eternity in her dove-filled attic when their youth suddenly drains away. John suffers this abrupt ageing and tries to seek help from Dr Sarah Roberts, to no avail. He simply provides Miriam's next lover - Sarah is seduced and turned, her research finding a living experiment within her own body.

Tony Scott is keen to dismiss his feature debut as a pretentious popvideo film, surprising considering the film spawned a (belated) TV series and remains a firm favourite with genre aficionados. Undeniably pretentious, the raison d'être of the film is to provide a discourse about age and immortality amidst a constant stream of beautiful and disturbing images.

Scott is a master of the widescreen format and he wastes no opportunity to fill the frame with tightly composed images or spatial separation. Judicious use of sound and visual editing to foreshadow events enhance the fragility and fragmentary nature of immortal time and represent the heightened senses of the burgeoning vampirism in Sarah. Music plays a key role, from the opening gothic strains of *Bela Lugosi's Dead* (juxtaposing a savage monkey attack with seduction and murder), the elegiac *Miserei Mei* (during John's moving incarceration in one of many scenes reminiscent of Franju's masterpiece *Yeux Sans Le Visage*) and Delibe's delightfully Sapphic *Flower Duet* (first played diegetically by Miriam, it becomes a soundtrack for their lovemaking). Only Sarandon's make-up and clothing date the film, its timelessness extends even to the special effects work which is astonishing. The acting is uniformly superb, Deneuve the most alluring vampire since *Daughters Of Darkness* (to which the film is heavily indebted), Bowie tragic even in his Dr Phibes mask and Sarandon underplays the innocent object of Miriam's affection. *The Hunger* is also unusual in the fact that it does not derive its mythos directly from Stoker although it is no less vampiric. As slick, tight and profound as you want it to be and with an ending so horribly lyrical yet inevitable you really can't ask for more.

92min, 18, Warner Home Video, Fang Factor Five.

Fright Night (1985)

Dir: Tom Holland
St: Roddy McDowell, William Ragsdale

What do you do if there's a series of headless bodies turning up around town and you fear that your neighbour is the one responsible? For Charlie Brewster the suspicion that the murderer is also a vampire leads him to one man - Peter Vincent, washed-up TV horror presenter. Along with Amy they must convince the town of the existence of vampires and take on with the task of eradicating them.

An early example of the self-referential horror comedy that many seem to think started with *Scream* but in fact has been around almost as long as horror films themselves. All the elements are in place - even down to the hero knowing what's going on, but his mother inviting the vampire into the house anyway. Harder to contend with is a vampire wearing the worst jumper this side of Giles Brandreth, and that perennial teenage comedy figure Edward the Geek. Knowingly the exceptional prosthetics hark back to Lon Chaney's make-up on *London After Midnight* with their full entourage of incisors and a face-splitting Tasmanian Devil grin. There are a fair few chills along the way too, long fingernails scraping up the banisters, sudden appearances and a disco kidnapping. Yes they even manage a distressed damsel in the shape of Amy. It is all the right side of camp for things not to be dragged down into too much gross imagery with McDowell adding the right touch of drunken 50s authenticity. For all its taste-free New Romantic fashions, atrocious synth-pop muzak and Reaganite teenagers, *Fright Night* still manages to be an amusing and scary popcorn movie that deserved the attention it received. So successful it spawned two (inferior but still watchable) sequels.

102min,18, Cinema Club, Fang Factor Three.

The Lost Boys (1987)

Dir: Joel Schumacher
St: Keifer Sutherland, Jason Patric

Michael and his brother Sam have arrived in town and are keen to make new friends. What they don't want to do is end up with the local vampire community, who may be cool but are also the reason that their town is called the Murder Capital Of The World.

Based around the tagline "Sleep all day, party all night, never grow old and never die" and starring a bunch of pretty brat packers, this is probably the ultimate teen vampire movie. It's fast, loud and contains enough angst to satisfy the most hormonally challenged. The title borrows from Peter Pan, but that's about as far as the analogy goes. Like many Schumacher films, although the premise is promising, the execution doesn't quite deliver as satisfactorily as it could. There are a few great scenes, particularly the opening shot which shows the point of view of the unseen vampires' attack. The most interesting characters are Edgar and Alan Frogg, who run a comic store and happen to be vampire hunters in their spare time, but mainly it's teen stereotypes and little more. Passes the time.

93min, 15, Warner Home Video, Fang Factor Two.

The Monster Squad (1987)

Dir: Fred Dekker
St: Andre Gower, Ryan Lambert

100 years ago Van Helsing set about destroying evil, but blew it. Now Dracula has flown to America to get the magic amulet and tip the balance of power back to evil. Joining him is a resurrected mummy, a gillmonster, an angst-ridden wolfman, three vampire brides and Frankenstein's mon-

ster. Who can stop the incessant wave of evil crashing devastatingly into middle America? The Monster Squad, that's who! Formed to swap spooky tales, these plucky 12-year-olds have got the facts on anything esoteric. With Peter the dog and little sister Phoebe in tow (a bit of a blow to the macho gang but hey, she's the effective one) watch out monsters.

The thought of a bunch of kids doing *ET* and *Ghostbusters* impressions is not a particularly pleasant one, but *The Monster Squad* defies expectations by producing something that is funny, exciting and scary without resorting to saccharine. Some of the opticals look dated but all the monsters have been lovingly created from the original Universal horror films. Dracula's castle even comes complete with armadillos. The mummy looks like the original but when being unravelled the quality of modern prosthetic work shines. Similarly the wolfman, a stick of dynamite stuffed next to his, ahem, 'wolfdork' explodes only to reform in a dazzling display of sticky body parts - Stan Winston you are forgiven for *Zoltan*. The Count himself is a little uninspiring but very wicked and only Frankie remains a source of monster sympathy with some of the shots featuring Phoebe mirroring James Whale's classic. Without being condescending, its tongue is far enough in its cheek not to patronise, and is reverential enough to its sources not to outrage nostalgics. If, when the boys' teacher declares "Science is real, monsters are not" you feel like shouting "Oh yes they are" and cheer when a kid kicks a bad guy in the unmentionables, then this is for you.

78min, 15, 4-Front, Fang Factor Three.

Near Dark (1987)

Dir: Kathryn Bigelow
St: Adrian Pasdar, Jenny Wright, Lance Henriksen
Young framer Caleb is bitten by waif stranger Mae and joins a gang of nomads who ride throughout the Midwest, killing and destroying anything in their path. They are reluctant to accept Caleb and he in turn is unwilling to kill, although it soon becomes clear that he can no longer tolerate daylight and has developed an unhealthy appetite for blood. Will his wholesome father and sister be able to rescue him?

Near Dark is a refreshing kick in the (canine) teeth for Hollywood vampire flicks. For once the gift/curse of vampirism is not restricted to the aristocratic or privileged classes, but a bunch of obnoxious rednecks, who do exactly as they please. Lance, the leader, fought for the South in the Civil War, so it is quite clear where his politics lie. When they walk into a bar with the sole purpose of killing and destroying, they are bold, offensive and lethal. The kid, Homer, an odious little monster, drinks, smokes and uses his considerable cunning to kill his victims - it's unusual to have a child portrayed as pure unrepentant evil. The relationship between Caleb and Mae is key to the film - he becomes dependent on her, feeding from her open wrist. This first happens in an oilfield, the reciprocating pumps in the background a metaphor for both the sexual act and the bloodflow. Kathryn Bigelow has taken a lot of stick in the past for being a female director who makes high octane action flicks (clearly not very feminine, say the big boys), but she is an assured director who makes intelligent films that never fail to entertain. *Near Dark*'s techniques cannot be faulted. It is well paced, looks great (particularly the backlit shots of the vampires) and plays a new take on the vampire genre. Its only down point is an unconvincing conclusion.

90min, 18, Entertainment In Video, Fang Factor Four and a Red Neck.

Return To Salem's Lot (1987)

Dir: Larry Cohen
St: Michael Moriarty, Samuel Fuller

Hard-nosed anthropologist Joe Webber is pulled away from filming tribal sacrifices to look after his delinquent son at his deceased aunt's house in Salem's Lot. It comes as some surprise to later find his aunt still walking around and that most of the town are vampires. Rather than kill him they want him to document their behaviour and create a vampire bible for future generations. It soon becomes apparent that they are not being open about the documentary process and their reliance on cattle as a food source is a cover for more predatory nocturnal behaviour.

A typical Cohen film includes plenty of pace, invention and exploitation but with a political or social message should you want it. *Return To Salem's Lot* is no exception, effortlessly taking such weighty topics as class based capitalism ("vampirism and financial security go hand in hand"), police hypocrisy, age, fascism, AIDS, animal welfare and media voyeurism in its stride, while providing more than enough opportunity for squishy effects and latex gross-out. The addition of veteran provocateur director Fuller ("I'm not a Nazi hunter, I'm a Nazi killer") to the proceedings and a child who is not only a brat but cusses, smokes and has sex, is merely the icing on the cake. Stand-out scenes include the killing of two hobos by a troupe of giggling schoolchildren, a child wedding, a teenage punk being eaten by OAPs and the villagers hungrily snacking on anaesthetised cows to keep the human quota down - they later give up on the bovine diet and get a coach load of tourists in as a takeaway. While bearing no resemblance to Stephen King's stories, it acknowledges the mini-series by having the protagonist inherit "the Hooper's House on the hill." Sadly the terrifying Mr Barlow has been replaced by a towering bright blue Yoda lookalike, with the ability to crush a head in each spindly Muppet hand. What it lacks in suspense it makes up for in energy and nerve. The thinking person's splatter film.

96min, 18, Warner Home Video, Fang Factor Three.

Vampire At Midnight (1987)

Dir: Gregory Machlachi
St: Jason Williams, Gustav Vintas

The police are concerned about a series of murders called the Vampire Killings. Victor Radkof, a hypnotherapist, seduces young women and drains them of their blood. Roger is a cop infatuated (*Rear Window* style) with his neighbour Jennifer, who has become involved with Victor. Will Jennifer become a vampire? Will Victor be caught? Will Roger's goldfish survive?

This film is very bad. Its sickeningly 80s look, ideology ("I work with creative people and high achievers") and style combined with vacuous lighting, unimaginative camerawork and leg warmers add up to an excruciatingly dull experience. The characters are gormless stereotypes, there's no suspense and although it tries to follow the "seductive vampire" route, it is about as erotic as a fart. There is a twist, but by the time you've reached the end, it's doubtful you'd care.

88min, 18, Palace, Fang Factor One.

Dracula's Widow (1988)

Dir: Christopher Coppola
St: Sylvia Kristel, Joseph Sommer, Lenny von Dohlen

Raymond, who runs The Hollywood House Of Wax, is surprised to find an extra box of paraphernalia for his Dracula display. Inside one lies Vanessa, Dracula's widow, who makes Raymond her slave. Unsurprisingly, the hideous mutilation of a local gangster and group of devil worshippers does not go unnoticed, so hardened police inspector Hap Lanson is called onto the case to bore us to tears with his sub-Raymond Chandler style voiceovers.

Oh dear. A messy film in more ways than one, *Dracula's Widow* is flapping nowhere. Blessed with expert over-the-top lighting, the film then proceeds to throw it away with lacklustre cinematography and bland direction. The comic-book approach seems to be present to mirror the supposedly witty script but is dashed by some inappropriately graphic murders and an over tendency to focus on gruesome body parts. Incongruous in the extreme with a script fit for 50-minutes tops, it further insults by putting Kristel in a rubber Halloween mask. Presumably they had spent all their make-up budget on the dead rather than the living dead. Meaningless irising between scenes and a poor soundtrack compound the aggravation - too nasty, not funny and, biggest crime of all, not interesting.

86min, 18, Polygram, Fang Factor One.

Vampire's Kiss (1988)

Dir: Robert Bierman

St: Nicolas Cage, Jennifer Beal

Peter Leow is a literary agent and, to put it bluntly, thoroughly arrogant and offensive. He strings along his girlfriend Jackie and humiliates his employee Alva, because he can. After a drunken night of feeble fumblings, he finds himself unexpectedly aroused by a bat that intrudes on his activities. Before long he has a new lover, neck-gnawing Rachel, and our literary protagonist develops an aversion to mirrors, a penchant for dark glasses and takes to sleeping during the day underneath his upturned sofa. But is he really turning into a vampire?

American work ethic as vampirism in this wannabe art film, Cage's Peter Leow is a manic bastard of humungous proportions, a vampire before he meets the bat. Indeed it could be seen that he is delusional, using this as a way of diverting his guilt. Despite an aversion to light he seems physically unaffected by it and when faced with mirrors he shuns touching them but they reflect him perfectly. His disturbed behaviour is made more wince inducing because it feels strangely real. This could so easily have been a serious look at the modern workplace and relationship pressures, especially on exploited groups. Instead the message is all a bit cack handed and a touch overlong. But there is a monumental saviour to this, Cage himself. A truly outstanding performance that raises the film to sublime levels, he is genuinely insane. Wince as Cage eats a real cockroach - really, yuck! Gasp as he teaches the alphabet! Snigger as he dons plastic vampire teeth and tries to speak properly! He points his finger *Wild At Heart* style, jumps ferociously on tables, accosts people in toilets, rolls his wide eyes like a madman on angel dust and trashes anything in sight. Outstanding! But what those domestic violence mime artists are all about is anyone's guess...

99min, 18, Cinema Club, Film Factor Two, Cage Factor Five.

Howling VI: The Freaks (1990)

Dir: Hope Perello
St: Brendan Hughes

Ian is a loner who finds work fixing up a church. He's a werewolf but a "new man" sort of a werewolf. Also coming to town is Harker's 'World of Wonders and Freaks' run by the annoying and evil Mr Harker, in fact a nasty vampire with elf-like pointy ears. He kidnaps Ian, cages him as a freak and eventually gets him framed for murder. With the town against him and his only inside help from the pitiful Alligator Boy, Ian's prospects don't look good.

A series in decline after Dante's masterfully playful yet nasty classic *The Howling* there was a need to attempt something to revive the overripe corpse of a series. Apparently some bright spark came up with the idea of mixing *The Howling*, *Freaks* and *Vampire Circus* with abominable results. The rot starts when nothing happens at all for the first hour. And that nothing happens very blandly. The actors aren't even poor enough to be funny, which is always a bad sign and the poignant teddy bear symbolism is hackneyed. The effects would be laughable but they are too dull. Even when the 'climax' occurs you are more relieved that the film has finally finished than excited. The film's tag line is "It's time to howl again." We did - in agony.

96min, 18, Palace, Fang Factor One.

Bram Stoker's Dracula (1992)

Dir: Francis Ford Coppola
St: Gary Oldman, Winona Rider, Keanu Reeves, Anthony Hopkins, Tom Waits

In 1462 Vlad Dracul renounces God following the suicide of his beloved wife. After many centuries he decides to take residence in London, convinced that his solicitor Jonathan Harker's fiancée Mina is the reincarnation of his dead bride. Dracula leaves Jonathan in Romania, being fed upon by three voracious vampire lovelies while he swans about London, infecting Lucy and seducing prim Mina. Clearly something must give but, after centuries of torment and loneliness the Count is unwilling to depart without a fight.

Hyped to the max on its release, *Francis Ford Coppola's Bram Stoker's Dracula* was derided by critics. This is a pity because the film is as grandiose, melodramatic and operatic as its overblown title would suggest. Coppola attempts to mirror the book's style by emphasising the use of letters and diaries to convey the distance between the protagonists and the stretching of time between scenes. As such, to many, the film is contrived and pompous, lacking realism and burdened with insufferably hammy acting (Keanu Reeves' accent is so outrageously plummy he could set up business as a fruit merchant). By opening the film with Vlad's story the emphasis is placed upon Dracula as a tragic figure, portraying him as a patriotic hero so our sympathies lie with him despite the barbarity of his actions. Oldman relishes his role, from the gliding crimson-robed count with shadowed hands to dashing top-hatted aristocrat with blue-tinted glasses and come-hither eyes. The character only really comes apart when encountered in one of many bestial forms, although this dissipates our loathing for his actions. Visually the film is a masterpiece, the sumptuous set designs and glass paintings have a gothic fairy-tale look. Dracula's presence is often felt, his eyes melting into moonlit skies or flickering gaslight. However the real star of the film is Eiko Ishioka who designed the magical costumes - a triumph of opulence and colour that revels in the decadence of the setting, from Renfield's Burtonesque straitjacket (Tom Waits in a film robbing role) to Lucy's incredible bridal attire. *FFCBS's Dracula* is ultimately an operatic love story, spiced with lashings of blood and a fair slice of erotica that is as guilty a romance as it seeks to portray.

121min, 18, Columbia TriStar, Fang Factor Four and a torrent of Kensington Gore.

Buffy The Vampire Slayer (1992)

Dir: Rubel Kuzui
St: Kristy Swanson, Donald Sutherland, Rutger Hauer

Buffy, an irritating teenager with trashy friends, discovers that she is The Slayer - a general executioner of the undead. This does not sit well with her lifestyle or her education. Still, she does have Merrick to instruct her in the ways of slaying. This is pretty convenient because there are vampires in town and they have an eye on the local school as a fast food outlet…

Joss Whedon's justly successful television series, with its hip humour and scary situations, began life as a feature film. It's a miracle anyone greenlighted the subsequent series on the basis of viewing this unattractive and dull work. There is not a single likeable character amongst the whole sorry lot of them - they are all thoroughly despicable and venomously bitchy - and those are the good guys. The baddies do not fare much better - Hauer lazily hams everything up and the 'oh so funny' extended death throes of a staked vampire in the final credits are a juvenile bore. Buffy's prodigious kung-fu skills would not have a 5-year-old worried, let alone a 500-year-old, but as everyone else is as nimble as a sedated geriatric you hardly care. The effects are woeful, the scenery lit by what appears to be an amateur operatic society during a lean phase and the soundtrack laughable. Sutherland appears drunk most of the time but if that's the case fair play to the man, I'd want to be too if I were stuck in this travesty. Apparently part of Whedon's motivation for creating the television series was to exorcise the demonic way they had butchered his script so there is one very good reason for the film to have been made, but none to watch it. The finest roses grow from the smelliest manure.

81min, 15, Fox Video, Fang Factor One.

Innocent Blood (1993)

Dir: John Landis

St: Anne Parillaud, Robert Loggia, Anthony LaPaglia

Two things keep you going when you are immortal, food and sex. There are two rules - never play with your food and always finish it. Marie is a beautiful French vampire in America, but she does have some morals - she only goes for criminals and ensures that they don't rise again. That is until she is disturbed feeding on gangster boss Sal "The Shark" Macelli who rises from the dead and sets about creating the ultimate gang of undead mobsters, redefining the term "made man."

A slight return to the heady days of *American Werewolf In London*, *Innocent Blood* lacks the tight charm of the former film but retains enough of its quirkiness to sustain interest. Parillaud makes a great, occasionally enigmatic, vampire who devours her victims like a zombie rather than the delicate approach - her aversion to mirrors runs through the film but she is at her most vulnerable when offered garlic-laced seafood at Sal's. Loggia is great as Sal, a dry run for the seriously deranged Mr Eddie in *Lost Highway*, and he hams the performance without ruining the tone (this is after all part comedy). Landis knows how to keep everything moving at the right pace although he will insist on peppering his films with pointless car crashes and tacky strip joints that detract from the more thoughtful aspects. As a comedy this only supplies the odd chuckle, but when you are trying to throw everything at a film this is to be expected. Most of the enjoyment comes from the little bits, the ineffectual handcuffing, the casual shattering of a plaster cast, the *Long Good Friday* references rather than the crumbling bodies and gross morgue scenes. There are plenty of cameos for genre aficionados to have a cheap chortle at too - Dario Argento, Sam Raimi, Frank Oz and effects supremo Tom Savini all crop up. You also get to play 'name that movie' at many key moments - view it as a film and quiz in one. Fun, frothy and a bit of a mixed bag, nowhere near as bad as some would have you believe.

113min, 15, Warner Home Video, Fang Factor Three.

Interview With The Vampire (1994)

Dir: Neil Jordan

St: Tom Cruise, Brad Pitt, Antonio Banderas, Christian Slater, Kirsten Dunst

In modern day San Francisco, vampire Louis relates the history of his life to a young journalist. Turned by Lestat, Louis describes his transformation and subsequent inability to take human life, and how he and Lestat adopted a young girl Claudia. Her inability to grow up nourished a hatred for Lestat and eventually she killed him, with Louis' help. They travelled and chanced upon Armand and his coven in Paris. But after Claudia was destroyed for killing Lestat, Louis was destined to remain a solitary soul.

Interview With The Vampire, based on Anne Rice's best-selling novel, was destined to be huge, particularly with Hollywood heart throbs in the leading roles. It is beautifully designed and lavish throughout, from the sumptuous recreation of the Old South to the extravagant Théâtre des Vampires. The effects too are stunning, particularly Louis' revenge as he burns down the coven and destroys all within by decapitation. All the performances are surprisingly good, Cruise is convincing as the "snob who loved to hunt in society" and Pitt suitably tortured as Louis. The primary fault is that it is played so straight - it is very linear and the pacing is far too constant. Although it deals with some quite complex issues, particularly with respect to Claudia, the girl who would never grow old but never grow up, it doesn't really take them any further than is completely comfortable. The Théâtre des Vampires breathes some life into proceedings, as the audience gaze upon vampires pretending to be humans pretending to be vampires. Ultimately the film is finely crafted, but lacks the sweeping melodrama to make it a classic.

117min, 18, Warner Home Video, Fang Factor Three.

Vampire In Brooklyn (1995)

Dir: Wes Craven
St: Eddie Murphy

Despite running around for centuries, Max, the one remaining pure bred African vampire, inexplicably only has until the full moon to reunite with his soulmate. Snags? Rita is in Brooklyn, unaware of her lineage and, even worse, works for the police. Max turns petty larcenist Julius into his ghoul, then goes for the woo - he needs just one dance to turn Rita and one kill to keep her forever, unless Rita's police chum and reggae-club nosferatu expert Dr Zekos can do something about it.

Eddie Murphy's erratic success over the years has thrown up some oddities, and a similar assertion could be applied to 'crash and boom' director Craven. Their teaming was bound to be…interesting. Murphy ensures that the comedy keeps going by possessing characters to showcase his acting, whilst retaining the smooth aristocratic aloofness of Max. As in *Coming To America,* the disguises are expertly handled, with a great turn as alcoholic Preacher Pauley convincing the congregation that "Evil is Good." Sensibly Craven gets on with the horror aspect of the script and gives it his all. After a portentously overblown opening involving an ocean vessel smashing through the harbour, the pace settles in admirably with some moody lighting and gruesome discoveries. Max's first murders mirror Arnie's in *Terminator* - a 'rendered limb from limb' feeding leads him to comment later "No food, I've already eaten Italian tonight." Indeed the race card is emphasised throughout the film but not at the expense of plot, comedy or shocks. However it also plays with genre too with Julius having all the best lines: "You ain't gonna pull that *Blacula* shit on me" or on realising that Max needs to rest in a coffin "Haven't you heard of a futon?" By no means perfect, it's a touch overlong and the climax is a little disappointing, *Vampire In Brooklyn* nonetheless manages to entertain throughout with a pleasant blend of chuckles and chills. Pet owners beware though - Max has a bizarre sideline in frizzling dogs and shooting cats!

97min, 15, CIC Video, Fang Factor Three.

Bordello Of Blood (1996)

Dir: Gilbert Adler
St: Dennis Miller

Vincent the dwarf (we mention the fact as he's there purely for exploitation value) revives Lilith in the depths of South America. Back in the US of A, heavy metal yob Caleb goes missing and his sister Katherine, a publicist for a TV evangelist, hires PI Rafe Guttman to find him. But Caleb has gone to the local funeral home which is a front for Lilith's vampiric bordello. So it's down to Guttman and the Rev to close down the brothel with holy-water-filled water pistols and rescue the now captured Katherine.

There are heroes, anti-heroes, post-modern heroes and wankers. Guttman is the latter and he's by no means the only problem in this lamentable film. A spin off from the successful *Tales From The Crypt* series, the daunting array of Hollywood behind-the-camera big names seems at odds with the final product, until you realise they probably had little to do with the resulting mess. And what a mess it is - adolescent T&A with no threat or sensuality and acting that's uniformly bland and plastic. No attempt has even been made to credit Lilith with any of her legendary status - it's just a name they've lazily dragged up without thought, care or attention. Some decent effects, including Lilith French kissing Caleb's heart out and a few CGI-enhanced wounds, are rendered tedious by unremittingly average direction. The piece as a whole shows its origins - a 22-minute TV programme extended to feature length by the addition of female-only nudity and sticky effects. Safe toss for pubescent males.

82min, 18, CIC Video, Fang Factor One.

From Dusk Til Dawn (1996)

Dir: Robert Rodriguez

St: George Clooney, Quentin Tarantino, Juliette Lewis, Harvey Keitel

The notorious Gecko brothers are on the run and want to cross over into Mexico, so they kidnap a faith-free ex-priest and his kids travelling in a camper. The destination? The Titty Twister, not a family-friendly joint but hey, they only have to hang out there until dawn breaks. But it soon becomes abundantly clear that a large portion of the staff and clientele are hungry for blood.

Rodriguez brings his energetic style to this early script by co-star Tarantino and it bears the marks of his other films - people walking coolly towards the camera as buildings explode in the background, the desert road shots, the mariachi band (here shown playing corpses as instruments!), the love of 50s B-Movies and the crotch gun (*Desperado*). Add a lot of knowing humour, a few sly digs at Stone's *Natural Born Killers* and more gore than *Dawn Of The Dead* and you have a whole bundle of fun. Stupid fun admittedly. However there is a major caveat to all this - *From Dusk To Dawn* is a lad's film pure and simple. There is nothing for women to do here except be provocative or victims and this leaves a nasty taste. Tarantino's typically irritating performance is uncomfortable as he tortures and kills an innocent victim and becomes thoroughly unwholesome as we see his sexually deranged fantasies towards Juliette Lewis. Aside from this the film is really two pulp scripts tacked together which are adequate but can't be resolved, hence the lurch into vampire territory. This is a delirious splatterfest of such proportions its sheer stupidity is the only reason it avoided the censor's shears - phallic stakes are attached to pneumatic drills, water pistols filled with holy water for searing good effect and each leg of a table used to impale a squishy vamp. The effects are great when they stay within prosthetic territory but are remarkably poor if they stray into CGI - the morphing in particular is decidedly passé. The final tally is for a braincell-free ride that never drags, is gross yet funny but sadly is overburdened with its outdated attitudes.

103min, 18, Buena Vista, Fang Factor Two or Four, depending on taste and alcohol level.

Blade (1998)

Dir: Stephen Norrington
St: Wesley Snipes, Stephen Dorff

Blade, half human, half vampire is on a mission to rid the world of the undead, particularly a new 'lower class' breed, led by Frost who have broken away from their traditional lifestyle. They are now intent on excessive partying and eradicating all the stuffy vampire elders. Oh, and world domination.

It's easy to see how *Blade* was Hollywood's attempt at updating the vampire myth. A pulsing soundtrack accompanies a young victim into a rave at an abattoir where the undead dancers indulge in a bloodbath before Blade comes crashing in and dispatches a few. It sets the pace for a bloody, action packed romp where the vampires have a kind of die fast, live young existence. Their leader Frost is cool, manipulative, and out for a good time. Perhaps bitter that he is a "turned vampire" rather than "pure blood," he doesn't care for the elder vampires' rules when he has discovered a means to raise a Blood God, so goes about his mission with ruthless efficiency, whilst partying to the max. Blade, in contrast really doesn't have a very good time at all. Sure, he can walk in the daylight and has vampiric strength, but has to inject serum to stop his blood cravings - he's all tortured soul on a mission to avenge his existence. And he has grumpy old Kris Kristofferson to live with too. It's hardly surprising you tend to side with the vampires as they have a much better time. The action is energetic, including a good deal of swordplay (heavily borrowed from Hong Kong cinema), it's edited speedily and the pacing never drags. If there is one criticism, it lies with the computer-generated blood which is just not bloody enough, although there's plenty of it. Slick, solid, enjoyable Hollywood entertainment, with exemplary design.

115min, 18, Entertainment In Video, Fang Factor Four.

John Carpenter's Vampires (1999)

Dir: John Carpenter
St: James Woods, Daniel Baldwin, Sheryl Lee, Thomas Ian Griffith.

When all bar one of Jack Crow's slaying team are killed by a Master Vampire, Jack is determined to seek revenge. Consulting with the Catholic church, he learns that his nemesis is in fact the first ever vampire and he's on a mission to complete a ceremony. With chum Montoya, naive priest Father Adam and bitten prostitute Katrina on hand, will Jack manage to save the world from the ultimate vampire?

This is not so much a vampire film, more a John Carpenter film with vampires. James Woods is the archetypal hardened cynical hero - tough, cool and competent, he works for the establishment but plays by his own rules. Like all the great Carpenter leads he's been set up and has to do his own thing. He doesn't suffer anyone gladly and is quite happy to taunt and threaten in order to survive. The film feels great, a vampire Western with Leone-esque wide sweeping vistas, great use of deep red lens filters (the shots of the vampires rising from the earth at dusk are amazing) and of course, Carpenter's own expressive score. This is combined with some unusual means of slaying - stake 'em, then winch 'em out into the sun whereupon they combust, kicking and screaming. The main flaw is that although Griffith is a great looking and ruthless vampire, aside from the opening where he does some seduction and slaying, there isn't an awful lot for him to do apart from be chased by Jack. Indeed most of his activities are shown from his point of view as Katrina develops her psychic link with him. Maybe it was intended that the film focus on the slayer, but promising vampirism that doesn't really go anywhere is a tease. That said, always engaging, looks great and hell, it's a Carpenter film.

103min, 18, Columbia Tri-Star, Fang Factor Four.

From Dusk 'Til Dawn 2: Texas Blood Money (1999)

Dir: Scott Spiegel

St: Robert Patrick, Bo Hopkins

Five criminals shack up at the El Coyote hotel prior to a bank job. Two flaws in this ingenious plan - an army of cops are on their trail and Luther has done a hit-and-run-and-shoot job on a vampire bat, stupidly mentioning this to the barman of the Titty Twister. One by one the gang get turned but will this interfere with their intended plan? Nah.

The popularity of the original, particularly on video, led to the production of this prequel and a sequel. The posters loudly proclaim - "From Quentin Tarantino and Robert Rodriguez" - but it's the usual puff, Spiegel's film takes all the worst elements of the original and accentuates them to the point of disgust. Early on one character notes that the porno the gang are watching on television "is very low quality" - oh the irony of it all. Despite some inventive touches - the smeary red bat vision, sticky endings and cartoonish wipes - this film exists for one purpose alone, to let men watch women being brutally violated under the cover of entertainment. From the cynical opening, added to pad up the running time and give Bruce *Evil Dead* Campbell a quick buck, the intentions are clear. There are two people, a man and a short skirted woman, in a lift. The man is attacked by bats - quickly. Then, in a homage (we use the term sarcastically) to *The Birds*, the woman is savaged seemingly endlessly, the bats biting under her dress and between her breasts. It gets worse. Men die macho stunt deaths, being blown up or thrown off buildings, even the policemen get preferential electric cabling death or car-based mayhem, but the women are all violated. Nasty, cynical, misogynist crap.

84min, 18, Buena Vista, Fang Factor None.

Modern Vampires (1999)

Dir: Richard Elfman

St: Casper Van Dien, Rod Steiger, Udo Kier

Nico, The Hollywood Strangler, is unaware of the huge underground network of vampires led by The Count. Dallas, a morally confused vampire has returned to LA, much to the Count's chagrin. Van Helsing is on all their cases, finding help in the shape of YTS slayer Timebomb and his posse of over-enthusiastic reprobates.

Richard Elfman, brother of composer Danny, has managed to create a film brimming with good ideas, and a few poor ones, that somehow never gels. Dallas is a little too goody-two-shoes (he turned Van Helsing's son to help ease the pain of disability and Nico to allow her to escape from her abusive stepfather) but is the only clearly focussed character. When the vampires bite you get an exhilarating rush of images - a church, a rose, lightning - but ultimately it goes nowhere. More disturbing is the garbled race message - everyone seems distinctly xenophobic, especially the unlikeable Nico, Van Helsing is implicated in Nazi atrocities, the Count forbids black vampires and Van Helsing's Boyz are horrendous racial stereotypes. This probably sounds worse than it is, the incongruous barrage of concepts would inevitably show some poor choices, but what remains is the film's lack of focus which emphasises the sour aspects. Where it does succeed is in some lively vampiric leaps, a deliriously seedy bar with caged naked human food, a 115-year pregnancy ("I can feel him kicking") and some great throw-away lines ("Lets kill some people together real soon" replaces "Let's do lunch"). All the cast seem to be enjoying themselves, especially veteran vampire Udo Kier. If you can ignore the faults and accept the mercilessly brutal stakings you'll enjoy yourself, just don't expect coherence.

Fang Factor Two and a tipple.

From Dusk Til Dawn III: The Hangman's Daughter (2000)

Dir: P J Pesce

St: Sonia Braga, Danny Trejo

Ambrose Bierce encounters Esmerelda, daughter of a sadist hangman, on his way to Mexico. They are lured to a bar with the prospect of gold but, with a barman who actually looks older now than he does a 100 years later their prospects ain't looking too rosy.

After the travesty of Part Two you would probably give this a very wide berth but wait, *The Hangman's Daughter* turns out to be a really great little film. Mirroring the original structurally, we get no vampires until well in, and setting it during the revolution is a stroke of genius that allows Pesce to explore the surrealism of the scenery detached from modern considerations. This feels more like a Rodriguez film with dynamic, impatient camerawork and editing, but there is also a debt to Dali in the shooting of rock formations and Jodorowski's *El Topo* in some of the design and imagery. The cemetery is fantastic, as is the execution scene with its death masks and parades. In some respects you don't want them to go to the Twister because the exterior scenes are so arresting, the almost sepia tone adding to the period feel with more than the odd nod to Leone. However, go they must. The climax is a mass of inventive special effects that will leave you gasping. Yes, some of the prosthetics are a touch ropey but when the staking starts you believe the wood is going through. It's all jolly tasteless with ripped open abdomens spewing forth armies f bats, but it works. Returning to its Mexican roots was the best thing that could've happened to the franchise. There's even a guy in a Santo mask!

94min, 18, Buena Vista, Fang Factor Three.

Resource Materials

Books

The Illustrated Vampire Movie Guide by Stephen Jones, Titan Books, ISBN 1-85286-449-4

This is a must have. Including far more many movies that can possibly be mentioned here, this is the book for the completist. Some of the references are a bit tenuous, but it's well illustrated throughout and a vital starting point for any enthusiast.

Dracula The First Hundred Years, Ed: Bob Madison, Midnight Marquee Press Inc, ISBN 1-887664-14-9

Fascinating and eclectic look at Dracula, this is a series of essays which covers not only films, but literature, comic books and other media.

The Aurum Film Encyclopaedia Horror, Ed: Phil Hardy, Aurum Press, ISBN 1-85410-384-9

Covering not only vampire films, but the entire horror movie genre, this is the definitive (and heavy) reference guide. Absolutely essential for horror buffs.

VideoHound's Vampires On Video by J Gordon Melton ISBN 1578590027

The VideoHound series are a great set of books which delve into particular genres, providing capsule reviews and saluting particular personalities. The edition on vampires is no exception.

Immoral Tales by Pete Tombs and Cathal Tohill, Titan Books, ISBN 1852866616

Excellent and well-illustrated source of information on European horror films, with extensive sections on Rollin, Franco and Borowczyk amongst others. Highly recommended. Also recommended is **Mondo Macabro** (Pete Tombs) which features bizarre films from around the world.

Bloodstone

The magazine for vampires, this is a fascinating and eclectic look at all aspects of vampirism and vampire related media. Brilliantly produced, but may contain some material suitable for adults only.

Internet

As you can imagine there are hundreds of sites dedicated to vampirism in its many forms. The following have good sections relating to film and lots of links to other sites. Beware though, it can be a dark and confusing world out there and you may hit upon real vampires and bloodsuckers that may not be to your taste. Such sites normally have plenty of warnings, so if you're unsure about the content, don't go there.

Pathway To Darkness

www.pathwaytodarkness.com

This is a great site with references to all things vampiric. With oodles of sub-sections, you're bound to find something of interest, whether it be essays on literature and film or chats with other vamps.

The Vampyre's Film List

http://www.netaxs.com/~elmo/vamp-mov.html

This contains an extensive listing of vampire films from all over the world. Clicking on a particular title will take you to the Internet Movie Database (www.imdb.com) for more details.

Vampire Museum

http://www.cobweb.com.au/%7Epentup/int2.htm

Loads of vampire info including music, trivia and a rogues gallery. Go to the Theatrette to find articles related to film.

Contact the authors: If you would like to correspond with Michelle Le Blanc & Colin Odell, and give them some feedback on this Pocket Essential, you can send an e-mail to: colinandmitch@yahoo.co.uk

The Essential Library

If you've enjoyed this book try the following titles in the Pocket Essentials library:

New This Month:
Vampire Films by Colin Odell & Michelle Le Blanc
Stephen King by Peter Mann

Coming Next Month:
Steve McQueen by Richard Luck
Sam Peckinpah by Richard Luck

Also Available

Film:
Woody Allen by Martin Fitzgerald
Jackie Chan by Michelle Le Blanc & Colin Odell
The Brothers Coen by John Ashbrook & Ellen Cheshire
Film Noir by Paul Duncan
Terry Gilliam by John Ashbrook
Heroic Bloodshed edited by Martin Fitzgerald
Alfred Hitchcock by Paul Duncan
Stanley Kubrick by Paul Duncan
David Lynch by Michelle Le Blanc & Colin Odell
Brian De Palma by John Ashbrook
Orson Welles by Martin Fitzgerald
TV:
The Slayer Files: Buffy the Vampire Slayer by Peter Mann
Doctor Who by Mark Campbell
The Simpsons by Peter Mann
Literature:
Noir Fiction by Paul Duncan

Available at all good bookstores at £2.99 each, or order online at **www.pocketessentials.com**, or send a cheque to: **Pocket Essentials (Dept VF), 18 Coleswood Rd, Harpenden, Herts, AL5 1EQ, UK**

Please make cheques payable to 'Oldcastle Books.' Add 50p postage & packing for each book in the UK and £1 elsewhere.

US customers should contact Trafalgar Square Publishing, tel: 802-457-1911, fax: 802-457-1913, e-mail: tsquare@sover.net